MW00334580

SEASONS OF CHANGE

SEASONS OF CHANGE

REFLECTIONS ON A HALF CENTURY AT SAINT LOUIS UNIVERSITY

BY

PAUL C. REINERT, S.J.
PAUL SHORE

SAINT LOUIS UNIVERSITY PRESS

© 1996 by University of Saint Louis Press

Library of Congress Cataloging-in-Publication Data

Reinert, Paul C. (Paul Clare), 1910–
    Seasons of change : reflections on a half century at Saint Louis
University / by Paul C. Reinert, Paul Shore.
        p.   cm.
    Includes bibliographical references (p.) and index.
    ISBN 0–9652929–0–8
    1. Reinert, Paul C. (Paul Clare), 1910–   . 2. St. Louis
University—Presidents—Biography.   I. Shore, Paul J., 1956–
II. Title.
LD4817.S517R45   1996
378.1'11'092—dc20
[B]   96–28829
                                                                   CIP

Marketing and Distribution:
Fordham University Press
University Box L
Bronx, New York 10458

PRINTED IN THE UNITED STATES OF AMERICA

CONTENTS

FOREWORD

Paul Reinert has accomplished many things in the past half century. I have been lucky enough to be a witness to some of his most remarkable achievements, and since he and I were in the same profession of university president for so many years, I have an especial appreciation for what he has been able to do, both for Saint Louis University and for education in general. Some of the most memorable incidents from his career will be told in the following pages, but Paul Reinert's greatest accomplishments are still worth mentioning here. Father Reinert led and sustained a Catholic urban university through a period of redefinition and growth, during which its relation to that community and its mission of service were amplified and enriched beyond anyone's expectation. When other institutions fled a city that was facing crisis, Paul Reinert and Saint Louis University stayed to fight and win the good fight, an endeavor which continues today. While maintaining the Jesuit traditions of academic excellence and liberal education, Father Reinert was able to reach out to people in all walks of life and invite them into meaningful participation in the life of the university. This participation benefited not only the university, but also those who learned from him how to give of themselves. He has always kept before himself and before those who worked with him the ideals of continual spiritual and intellectual development and service, never sacrificing the one goal for the other.

Paul Reinert has done more than this, though. By making Saint Louis University a model of how contemporary American Catholic higher education can confront the challenges of modern life, he provided leadership to countless other Catholic educators trying to find their way in the uncharted territory of life after Vatican II. His ability to maintain the meaningful Catholicity of the university while consciously broadening the university's constituency helped inspire the formulation of the ground-breaking Land O' Lakes statement and encouraged other educators throughout the country to clarify their own goals and values. The continuing success of Saint Louis University on all levels is testimony to the wisdom of Paul Reinert's vision.

I cannot limit this Foreword to a mere recitation of the man's accomplishments, however, for Paul Reinert is also a personality—a model, in the oldest and best sense, of tremendous energy, compassion, intelligence, and Christian humility—who would be remarkable if he had been the leader of no more than a parish Sunday school. His optimism and resourcefulness have won over many to his point of view, but probably just as many have been won by his honesty, his sincere belief in his mission, and his faith in God and the goodness of people. This book is in part for his friends who know these qualities and love him for them. Perhaps more importantly, however, this book is also for those who have not had the privilege of knowing Paul Reinert. For them this book will provide a glimpse into the life of a remarkable man, an admirable Christian, and a wonderful Jesuit priest.

(Rev.) Theodore Hesburgh, C.S.C.
President Emeritus
University of Notre Dame

INTRODUCTION

This book is an outgrowth of conversations between the two of us which took place during a nine-month period in 1994 and 1995. As is often the case in writing a book, the actual intent and direction of the work evolved somewhat over time. At first we were concerned principally with recording some of the most significant events which had occurred at Saint Louis University over the last five decades, with special emphasis on the experiences and perspective of Father Reinert. As we progressed, however, it became increasingly clear that merely to collect reminiscences about the development of the University would leave out a crucial part of the story: the "what" would be there but the "why" would not. What began, then, as essentially a historical reflection soon contained passages dealing with the philosophy of education, and specifically with Jesuit higher education.

As the focus of the book broadened, we had to consider how to meld the sometimes diverse components into a comprehensible whole. Gradually, several "voices" emerged. The personal recollections of Father Reinert, which, we believe, deserve to be retained in their original form, appear generally in the first person singular in italicized sections. A less personal historical narrative, which provides the connecting links for much of the book, is written in the third person. Our biggest challenge was to decide how to record the results of our conversations which focused on the philosophy of higher education. To use the third person seemed both to blunt the impact of these dialogues and also to suggest that these ideas had their inception in the mind of a long-dead individual who had lived in some distant historical context. Relating them in the first person singular, as the personal recollections are recorded, also did not do justice to the conversational give and take

ix

which we went through to get them on paper. We decided therefore to write the more philosophically oriented chapters in the first person plural.

The result is a somewhat unconventional format for a book, but then this book is itself unconventional—part personal recollection, part reflection based on long experience, and part philosophical observation and speculation about the future. In a small way, this book endeavors to reflect the continuing evolution of one university within both a Catholic and broader cultural context. Our choice of title, *Seasons of Change*, also reflects our desire to convey the dynamic but productive tension between the preservation of tradition and the adaptation of older institutions to new circumstances. The seasons change, but they are also recurring events, for each time that a unique spring comes, it recapitulates all earlier springs. As Catholic higher education grapples with the questions of what are its essentials and what are merely accidentals of time and place, it must confront both unique and cyclic elements in its development, with hope and faith, and with doubt and conflict, and competing aspirations and objectives. Much of this book attempts to deal with these problems, with solutions which were found and with well-intended tries which failed. It is not a triumphal narrative, but rather, we hope, an honest account of the development of the identity of a modern urban, Catholic university, a development which will never cease as long as the university survives. We confess to a more didactic purpose to this book, too. We believe that universities must strive to resist control from government, from business, or from narrow sectarian domination. Yet all colleges and universities must deal with all these entities, and Saint Louis University is no exception. The task of interpreting the university to these entities, finding common ground for concerted action while still retaining the freedom which is the lodestar of American higher education, is a recurring theme here. We hope that the intended purpose of each of these components is clear to the reader, and that some of our experience of discovery and rediscovery in the writing of this book will be shared by others.

A number of people deserve thanks for making this project possible. Dr. Richard Breslin, executive vice president and provost of Saint Louis University, Dr. Alice Hayes, former executive vice president and provost of Saint Louis University, and Dr. Donald Brennan, dean of the Graduate School, supported this project morally and materially. Rev. Richard W. Rousseau, S.J., of the Consortium of Jesuit University

Presses, graciously arranged much of the logistics for the production of this, the first book produced by Saint Louis University Press, and offered wise counsel in the design of the book. John Waide and Randy McGuire of the Saint Louis University Archives were instrumental in assisting with the verification of historical facts as well as in the researching and printing of the photographs used in this book. Mary Bruemmer and Dan Schlafly aided in recalling events from years past. Lisa Graham and Melanie Zamachaj provided invaluable assistance in editing and research. Linda Lashley and Pat Murphy aided with typing and secretarial support. Paul Shore's wife, Ilene, also deserves thanks for her insightful suggestions and reactions to the manuscript as it developed.

Saint Louis   Paul C. Reinert, S.J.
November 1995   Paul Shore

CHAPTER

ONE

BEGINNINGS

Train up a child in the way he should go, and when he is old, he shall not depart from it.

—Proverbs 22:6

The First Thirty Years

One morning in the 1880s on an immigrant boat bound for America, four German brothers were discussing their hopes and plans for their future in the new land. They were all from a small village, Tünsdorf in the Ruhr district, and they had all been trained as tailors, the occupation their father had followed. Once they reached their new home, they did not want to be in competition with one another as tailors, so they reasoned that it would be best if they went to different parts of the country to seek their fortunes. Perhaps not completely realizing how large the new land to which they were headed actually was, they decided that they would all head to different states, and put the names of some of the states they knew into a hat. Each brother drew a name out of the hat. Martin, one of the brothers, drew the name Iowa, and so was soon heading to Sigourney, Iowa, where he started a tailoring business in 1886 and married a local girl.

After twenty years in Iowa, Martin's pioneering spirit attracted him to follow the "gold-rush" trail, and he founded a men's clothing store in the town of Boulder, Colorado. Once established, Martin persuaded one of his younger brothers, John, to move to Longmont, Colorado.

Thus, at the turn of the century, a series of Reinert Clothing Stores advertised as "The Hub" came into existence. Martin Reinert had two children, Francis and Marie. Son Francis married Emma Voegtle, and despite a strong desire to become a professional baseball player (not an entirely reputable calling in the early 1900s) followed in his father's career at the clothing store. Francis and Emma had six children, all boys. The eldest, born on August 12, 1910, was named Paul. Boulder was then a small college town with a population of about 8,000 and only one Catholic Church. The growing Reinert family lived across the street from the Church and was one of the more prominent families in the parish. Francis was a gregarious man who could mix comfortably with any class of society, while Emma was quieter, but revered by her boys for her character and religious ideals. Ultimately, three Reinert boys would become Jesuit priests, and two of these would become presidents of Jesuit institutions of higher learning. But such developments were not yet apparent as Paul Reinert was growing up.

Fr. Reinert recalls himself as a "mountain boy," loving the Colorado outdoors and, like his father, addicted to sports, including fishing. He did well in school, but he attributes this to his "inheritance" rather than to any passionate desire to become a scholar, let alone an educator. At thirteen, after attending Sacred Heart parochial school in Boulder, he traveled thirty miles south to Denver, where he became a boarder at Regis High, a school run by the Jesuits. Life at Regis was in many ways austere. The curriculum, in the best Jesuit tradition, stressed the classics, and the boys slept in a large, spartanly furnished dormitory, the beds separated from one another only by curtains. On some Colorado winter mornings the water in the washbasins was frozen. But there were many good times at Regis as well. Living with the high school students were Jesuit scholastics, young men who had not yet completed their training and who were serving as teachers for three years. Many of these scholastics were athletes, and coached as well as played sports with the boys. Paul Reinert lettered in three sports: basketball, football, and baseball, and dreamed of going on to college on a football scholarship.

The Reinert family was prosperous enough to provide career

opportunities to its sons exceeding those to which many families of the 1920s could aspire. Carl, four years younger than Paul, became a Jesuit and later served as the president of Creighton University in Omaha. John Francis became the heir apparent of the business and worked in the store until his untimely death in 1965 at the age of 42. George, the next son, attended Regis High School and College in Denver, and after serving as a fund-raiser for his alma mater, became vice president for development at St. Joseph's Hospital in that city. Since then he has also been a professional development officer for several dioceses in Arizona and California, as well as serving as an ordained deacon in his parish church. James also entered the Society of Jesus and became a principal of Kapaun High School in Wichita. Later he served as assistant principal at Saint Louis University High School, assistant provincial for the Missouri Province, and spent the last fourteen years of his life as chaplain at Cardinal Glennon Hospital for Children. The youngest child, Robert, died of peritonitis at the age of seven.

In the light of such a rich religious family heritage, it might be easy to say that Paul Reinert's choice of a life vocation was natural, if not inevitable. But for the Colorado teenager none of this was yet obvious. Paul, who had not been drawn to a career in the family store and had considered becoming an attorney, did not envision himself as a future priest. When Fr. Francis O'Hern, dean of men at Saint Louis University, came to Regis to give a retreat and talked to the seniors about choosing a career, and even about considering entering the Society of Jesus, Paul, as he recalls, "kind of fought it." He went to see Fr. O'Hern to tell him that he did not appreciate being pressured into a vocation. O'Hern did not argue with him, but mentioned that Paul's best friend, Dan Campbell, had decided to enter the novitiate in Florissant, Missouri, to see if the priesthood was for him. Paul raced out to find if it was true. It was, and after a good deal of soul-searching both seniors decided that they would go to Missouri and enroll at St. Stanislaus Seminary together.

This decision was both harder and easier than such a move would be now, which explains why the Society seldom recruits from high schools today. Choosing to enter the priesthood was more difficult then because vows were truly perceived as binding and permanent. The phenomenon of the former priest was virtually unheard of, and the rigors of preparation for the priesthood were considerably more demanding than they are in the 1990s. On the other hand, there were some distinct advantages to embarking on a career in the Society in those days. Since many young men entered the novitiate together from the same high school, the sense of loneliness that a single novice would encounter was greatly reduced. Entering a religious order with a corporate identity as opposed to the isolation of parish work was another advantage for many novices. Then, too, for the majority of the families from which the novices came, having a son who was a priest was a source of great pride. Yet when Paul Reinert and Dan Campbell were about to enter the novitiate, they concocted a story that they had both received football scholarships to the University of Kentucky. After a brief visit with Dan's sister at the Loretto Novitiate in Nerinx, Kentucky, the two supposed future gridiron heroes started west again, arriving at St. Stanislaus Seminary in Florissant to begin classes on September 1, 1927.

The program of training leading into incorporation in the Society of Jesus and eventual ordination is a long and strenuous one. The first step was a two-year novitiate where novices received spiritual training and engaged in a good deal of soul-searching to determine if the life of a Jesuit was truly for them. Under the demanding tutelage of Fr. Leo Krenz, a former diocesan priest, the novices were put through their paces—and there were several times when Paul was advised that he might not be cut out to be a Jesuit. Nevertheless, Paul Reinert did not wash out, and like the approximately fifty percent of the other novices, completed his training and pronounced his first vows as a Jesuit in 1929. The Juniorate followed. This was a two-year, heavily academic program at the college level, including modern and classical languages, literature, and other courses such as archeology.

Then followed the big move from the country to Grand and Lindell Boulevards in St. Louis for a three-year program concentrating heavily on Thomistic philosophy. If a Jesuit Scholastic had by that time been assigned to a major field of specialization, appropriate courses were also taken during these three years. As a result, Reinert, by 1934, had completed both a licentiate (an ecclesiastical degree) in philosophy as well as a master's degree in education, the latter being a first step toward his advanced training for administration in higher education.

The thirteen-year, highly structured training then prescribed a three-year stint in teaching at one of the Jesuit high schools in the Missouri Province. In the fall of 1934, Reinert found himself reporting to the legendary principal of Creighton University Preparatory School, Fr. Henry (Heinie) Sullivan in Omaha, Nebraska. There he taught Latin and Greek and served as athletic director and moderator of the Prep Theater's performances. Added was an emergency assignment for which he was totally unqualified: teaching a special course in social studies for a group of seniors, mostly football players, who needed extra credits in order to graduate on time.

The lockstep Jesuit formation program next prescribed four years of heavy concentration on theology and canonical preparation for ordination and the ministries of the priesthood. Up to 1937, Missouri Province Scholastics had returned to the Saint Louis University campus for this climactic phase of their training. But Reinert's class was commissioned to a major change in locale and environment—to the windswept plains of Kansas where stood the empty buildings that had previously housed both St. Mary's Jesuit High School and College. This once-prosperous institution had fallen victim to the ravages of the Depression and the dust-bowl days.

The four isolated years at St. Mary's were rewarded by the long-awaited ordination to the priesthood on June 26, 1940, by Archbishop Schulte, the second oldest living graduate of Saint Francis College in Quincy, Illinois (the oldest being Paul's father Francis), now called Quincy University.

The rural retreat in Kansas came to an abrupt end when in the summer of 1941 Fr. Reinert enrolled as a doctoral student at the University of Chicago. There Fr. Reinert experienced a great change from the rural isolation of Kansas. He resided at Holy Cross parish rectory, which was in the middle of bustling south-side Chicago where racial and ethnic tensions had been heightened by World War II jitters and restrictions.

THE CHICAGO YEARS

In the 1940s the University of Chicago had already come to be recognized as one of the great universities of the United States. Located on the former site of the 1893 World's Fair on the south side of the city, and boasting one of the most ambitious and best funded research programs anywhere, the University attracted students and scholars from throughout the world. Among these students was a small contingent of American Jesuits training for academic and administrative posts at their colleges and universities. The experience in Chicago provided the young priest with, in effect, two educations: one academic and another based on the realities of American urban life. Both experiences profoundly affected Fr. Reinert's philosophy of education and his vision of what a university should be.

While the wartime University of Chicago boasted a number of commanding intellectual figures, the campus was dominated by the personality of its president, Robert Maynard Hutchins. Hutchins, who served as president from 1929 to 1945, set out to make the University a bastion of liberal education and scholarship in the midst of a society increasingly influenced by mass popular culture. More than that, Hutchins also served as a spokesman for the ideals of rigorous academic standards at all levels of schooling and for exacting scholarship in lectures, radio broadcasts, and other public forums. The university that Hutchins sought to create was, despite its debt to European intellectual traditions, distinctively American, committed to the opportunities afforded by democracy and to the idea of providing an education formerly reserved for the elite to any who could qualify for admission. Among Hutchins' most characteristic reforms were his decision to admit students as young as fifteen to the undergraduate college, provided they could pass the entrance exam, and his elimination of the football team. His university was to be a meritocracy designed to serve the republic by producing intellectual leaders, not a community service institution or a source of entertainment.

Fr. Reinert attended lectures by Hutchins and by Mortimer Adler, another bearer of the torch of academic excellence, who later developed the widely used Great Books curriculum. Adler had noted that the word "school" was derived from the Greek word *schole*, meaning leisure, specifically the leisure which the Greek aristocrats utilized to expand their intellects. He asserted that universities should focus exclusively on the development of the intellect and teach nothing of a purely vocational nature. To a large degree the University of Chicago followed this philosophy. All around him Fr. Reinert found the brightest of the bright: high school valedictorians; graduate students who had had brilliant undergraduate records; dedicated, able, and in many cases, highly idealistic youth from privileged backgrounds. Adler, Hutchins, and other University of Chicago instructors strove to bring to these students a demanding curriculum that raised serious philosophical questions and excluded mundane or practical problems. One day there would be a lecture on a particular book or theme, and the next day the instructor would "take apart" a student by calling on him or her and firing a series of probing questions derived from the previous day's lecture. Examinations were exacting and intimidating. The atmosphere in the lecture halls and elsewhere on campus was deliberately and, on occasion, self-consciously intellectualist, stressing at the same time individual development and immersion in the works of the great thinkers of the past. As he watched the classroom debates and the scholarly efforts of undergraduates and graduates, Fr. Reinert found himself wondering what would happen to these young scholars when they left the confines of the university and entered the outside world. While it was clear that the sort of training Chicago provided was broadening the vision of many a freshman who had never before been compelled to analyze long-accepted beliefs, there was an inevitable gap between the perspectives of these rigorously trained students and those held by most of the rest of society. The difference in perspectives went far beyond the number of books read or lectures attended, and was really a difference in values. To Fr. Reinert it seemed likely that the day-to-day concerns of ordinary people would bore or repel some graduates, while the graduates themselves would seem to the surrounding community aloof and ill-prepared for a useful life. Such a division between the *vita contempletiva* and the *vita activa* is as old as higher education itself, but in a rapidly changing and socially stratified society which nevertheless aspired to being a democracy, this failure to provide students contact with the outside world appeared to Fr. Reinert an especially glaring omission. Other aspects of the University's academic life made lasting impressions on him. Courses in administration and the social sciences often stressed what seemed to Fr. Reinert excessively dry and irrelevant research, and, as is often the case, the greatest published experts in a number of areas did not always turn out to be brilliant teachers. Fr. Reinert's fellow graduate students, many of whom were experienced administrators, in general appeared to accept the status quo. Graduate programs enabled students to produce critiques of social conditions, but it seemed to Fr. Reinert that the more important business of creating solutions was given less attention. It did not seem likely that decisive change in either education or society would result from the research students were compelled to do, or which professors were producing.

Yet change was coming to the University of Chicago from another direction: the surrounding community. The 63rd Street area, which had been a very secure middle-income neighborhood, began to deteriorate rapidly during the war years. Poor people, both African American and white, were moving in, and what had been single-family homes became boarding houses or apartments. Businesses along the Midway Plaissance and in other parts of Hyde Park moved out. Established Catholic parishes found that their new neighbors were not Catholic and also left. Long-time residents, exhibiting a pattern that would be repeated over and over again in the postwar era, panicked and moved, bringing about dramatic, almost overnight shifts in the composition of neighborhoods. The University of Chicago also reacted to the sudden changes in its environment, and set out to protect itself from further encroachment by buying up every piece of property it could find and turning the campus into a fortress, now not simply of the mind, but of the body as well. This process of deliberate isolation, and the inevitable hostile reaction of the community to an educational institution that seemed to want to have nothing to do with it, convinced Fr. Reinert that the university was continuing in its failure to fulfill a major obligation to society. He felt that the definition of a university as an institution with primary objectives of teaching and research was inadequate. He was uncomfortable with the message put out by Chicago and by many other leading U.S. universities that some community service on the part of the faculty was acceptable but there was a great danger in allowing the faculty to become too involved in the political and social concerns of the community. Not only did such a viewpoint fail to square with the Ignatian vision of education, but it also seemed out of step with need of the ever broadening segment of the population from which university students were being drawn. The model which placed scholarship first had been born in the universities of nineteenth-century Europe, and especially in Prussia, where only a tiny fraction of the population had any hope of ever attending a university and where social problems were not viewed as the legitimate concern of any educational institution. Such a philosophy did not seem to Fr. Reinert either achievable or appropriate for an urban institution in an increasingly diverse democracy.

The University of Chicago, of all the visible examples of a university, was the greatest single influence on Fr. Reinert's philosophy of higher education, but it was not the only one. Another model, which existed on the printed page if not in the material world, was also important in shaping his views. This was Cardinal Newman's *Idea of a University*. Newman, although trained at Oxford in as rarefied intellectual atmosphere as could be found at Chicago, sought to develop a philosophy of education which was both holistic and in many ways traditional, but which concentrated on developing the "habits of the mind" in preparing a student for future engagement with the issues of the industrial revolution.

Newman's vision of the university, in addition to having a religious base, also placed great stress on the unifying principle of the institution. Whereas Clark Kerr a century later would speak of the "multiversity," an institution whose various parts could be added or subtracted without injury to the institution as a whole, Newman viewed the university as an organic whole, having indeed as much or more of a corporate identity than Medieval universities. While it might have been natural for a product of a Jesuit university such as Fr. Reinert to favor the more holistic view of Newman, it was still the case that in the 1940s larger American universities were moving toward a more fragmentary view of themselves. Patterns of research funding, the continuing growth of independent professional schools, and the increasing diversity of the student body all promoted the notion of a fragmented university. By contrast Fr. Reinert's unity of vision would translate into a unified approach to curriculum, to the position that Saint Louis University would take on moral and social issues, and to the product of the institution—the students.

It would be easy to misconstrue the idea of a unified mission for the university as a narrow set of concerns, a perspective confined to a small geographical area, a curriculum that made too few allowances for growth in the body of human knowledge, and a reluctance to reach out to other segments of the community. Nevertheless, under the right circumstances and with leadership committed to Newman's ideal, the vision could become more than a dream.

THE FIFTY YEARS AT SAINT LOUIS UNIVERSITY BEGIN

With the completion of his doctoral work in Chicago in the summer of 1943, Fr. Reinert still had a final full year of Jesuit formation to complete. This intensive year of prayer, study of the Constitutions of the Society of Jesus, initial opportunities for preaching, giving of retreats, etc., took place at a seminary in Parma, a suburb of Cleveland, Ohio. With Tertianship (the sixteenth year of preparation since he began Jesuit training) completed, Fr. Reinert arrived at Saint Louis University in the summer of 1944 presumably to serve as an apprentice assistant dean to the highly regarded Fr. Wilfred Mallon. Fr. Reinert was shocked to learn that in midsummer Fr. Mallon had been transferred to the key position of director of studies for the Missouri Province. Instead of an apprentice, Fr. Reinert was now dean of the College of Arts and Sciences; the president of the University, Fr. Patrick Holloran, soon reminded him: "You're responsible for the successful management of two new and immense problems: integrating black students into our undergraduate program, and providing added faculty, classrooms, etc., for several thousands of GIs who are headed this way." While neither of these challenges seemed trivial, the implications of both stretched far beyond what could have been foreseen in the closing days of World War II. Expansive changes in the mission and vision of Saint Louis University, in the surrounding city, and in the very character of American higher education lay ahead. It is to these changes that we now turn.

CHAPTER

TWO

CHANGE

A JESUIT UNIVERSITY MUST BE OUTSTANDING IN ITS HUMAN, SOCIAL, SPIRITUAL AND MORAL FORMATION. . . .

—DECREES OF GENERAL CONGREGATION 34 OF THE SOCIETY OF JESUS, DECREE 17, NUMBER 414

Fr. Paul Reinert arrived at Saint Louis University in 1944 to serve as dean of the College of Arts and Sciences, with World War II still far from over, and with the postwar transformation of American society only dimly foreseen by a few. Half a century ago St. Louis was a racially segregated city in virtually all aspects. There were separate schools, streetcars, restaurants, theaters, and public restrooms throughout the city. There were even separate publicly supported teachers' colleges. Stowe College, a blacks-only institution, was located in St. Louis on North Kingshighway. Harris College, located a few blocks from the Saint Louis University campus, was for whites. Both colleges were operated by the Saint Louis City public schools. (The two schools were merged into the state system of higher education in 1954 to form Harris-Stowe State College, which still operates.) Segregation even followed black St. Louisans to the grave.

11

When African Americans became ill, they went to a segregated hospital. When they died, they were often buried in a segregated cemetery. Although Saint Louis University was located in a racially mixed section of the city, in 1944 it was still an all-white institution, and it was rare for an African American even to be seen walking across the campus. This was all the more remarkable considering the area in which Saint Louis University was located. When the University had relocated from its original downtown location to Grand Avenue after the Civil War, the surrounding neighborhoods had been among the city's finest. Through the "Gaslight Era" and into the first part of this century, the neighborhood continued to be a vibrant combination of stately homes, motion picture houses, ice cream parlors, and respectable boarding houses. By the 1940s, however, the area east of Grand was losing its middle to upper class residents, who were moving to the western part of the city or to St. Louis County, leaving the district east of Grand Avenue to fester until it gained a reputation as one of the worst slums in the United States. The area's residents, many of them black, had virtually no contact with the University's campus, and on the other hand, undergraduates were told to avoid the crime and brothels east of Grand. Poor whites, many from the hill regions of the South and disparagingly referred to as "Okies," also lived east of the campus. Communication between town and gown in general was poor.

Although Saint Louis University was over one hundred years old, its reputation in St. Louis was not an accurate reflection of reality. To many in St. Louis, the University was regarded as little more than a Catholic seminary, or an extension of the parochial school system. Many citizens, including prominent business leaders (few of whom were Catholic), did not even know that Saint Louis University had non-Catholic students and instructors, or that it offered majors in non-religious subjects. Local Jewish high school graduates, for example, often assumed that they just were not welcome, and perpetuated the widely held assumption that Saint Louis University had only a narrow interest in the larger world. The University administration, while not adverse to having better relations with the community, had made little systematic effort to improve this image or to reach out to the community. History had played a role in this attitude. Saint Louis University, during the first decades of its existence, had been the subject of vicious attacks by anti-Catholics. A period of isolation had followed, and with the emergence of Washington University as a prestigious educational institution which attracted many of the city's most elite families, Saint Louis University had not played as highly visible a role in the life of the city as it had in its earliest history. An exception to this was the Medical School, which became a School of the University through the purchase of the Marion-Sims-Beaumont School in 1903, and the Education Department, which traced its history far back to the early days of the University and had trained a significant portion of the city's teachers and school administrators. The Business and Law Schools, however, were relatively low profile and both offered only evening classes which were not seen as competition to the professional schools of Washington University or the University of Missouri.

The end of World War II saw the beginning of one of the most dynamic periods of growth in American higher education. The G.I. Bill of Rights made a college education possible for millions of Americans who had never before had such an opportunity. The enrollment of colleges and universities, typically stagnant during the war years, skyrocketed. Enrollments rose dramatically at Saint Louis University, with an added feature: many of the new students were not Catholic, nor did they have the traditional career goals of the Jesuit university student. Veterans going back to school were a different breed. They were, of course, older, more often married than not, and with an outlook on life shaped by years of military service, travel, and the horrors of war. They wanted a practical education, and they wanted it in a hurry. While instructors enjoyed the commitment to a work ethic and the real life experience that the veterans brought to the classroom, Saint Louis University administrators sometimes despaired of persuading non-Catholic veterans of the importance of taking several semesters of philosophy or even other liberal arts classes. Veterans of Saipan or Anzio, while respectful of instructors, administrators, and fellow students, were less overawed with the experience of going to college than many eighteen-year-olds, and more likely to insist on their own agenda. These students, many of whom had passed through St. Louis during the war or had been stationed nearby, brought a new diversity to the institution, but they also placed strains, material and philosophical, on Saint Louis University. A basic problem was finding room for the flood of students who arrived after 1945. Quonset huts, for example, were used for classes in the College of Arts and Sciences immediately after the war. An annex to the Medical School, added in 1946, the purchase of

Cupples House, a Victorian mansion, and the addition of Parks College of Aeronautical Technology in 1946 were further evidence of not only the physical expansion of the University to accommodate the increased numbers of students, but also the widening vision of the mission of the University which developed in the postwar years.

WOMEN

The Ignatian conception of education, developed in the Renaissance, was in many ways revolutionary, but in some aspects it reflects the values and the assumptions of its time and place of origin. Nowhere is this more obvious than in its view, or perhaps non-view, of women in higher education. Sixteenth-century European universities did not admit women students, and the Jesuit-dominated universities which flourished in the following centuries continued this policy without question. As was true elsewhere, Jesuit educators did not so much fight to prevent the inclusion of women as much as they simply failed to acknowledge the existence of women in their plans. Even the painfully slow emancipation of women in the United States and the development of co-educational colleges and universities had little impact on the theory or practice of Jesuit higher education. An all-male religious order dedicated to the training of young men did not see the education of women as its responsibility.

When Saint Louis University had to respond to the women who sought education within its walls, it did so in a way that was both typically Jesuit and reflective of policies then followed throughout the country. The first women admitted to study at the University were graduate students. Following the example of Ivy League schools, individual women were allowed to complete advanced studies within the graduate school, but officially women were not to form any part of the undergraduate student body. Nevertheless, women were unofficially admitted for undergraduate study at Saint Louis University throughout most of the twentieth century.

University administrators had persistently requested permission from authorities in Rome to grant women admission to Saint Louis University, and when they had not been able to receive support from the Father General of the Society of Jesus, they had eventually worked out a circuitous solution. The case was made that good lay teachers and principals were badly needed in parochial high schools and grade schools, and that there were many able young women who wanted to teach and needed to be educated. A special School of the University, Education and Social Sciences, was therefore established in 1937 expressly for the North Campus women who wanted training as teachers and social workers. It was the result of the merging of the School of Education (founded in 1925) and what were formerly undergraduate courses in the School of Social Service. In 1942 its name was changed to "University College," a separate fictitious academic structure for women with its own dean, even though most classes were attended with the male students. The first dean of women, Nancy McNeir Ring, was appointed in 1943 and served in that capacity until 1967. University College existed until 1949, when it was combined with the College of Arts and Sciences.

Special arrangements were also made with the female religious orders whose members were not allowed to leave cloister in order to come to the University. For example, among the women religious who were pursuing Ph.D.s in a variety of subjects was Mother Marie Kernaghan, RSCJ. at Maryville College, who received a Ph.D. in physics in 1929 under the direction of Fr. James Shannon, chairman of the physics department.

As we have already noted, women were able to attend Saint Louis University in the 1940s through a method of subterfuge whereby they were designated members of University College. By the late 1940s, the fiction of University College had been replaced with the formal admission of women to the University as students in good standing, even though the University's graduate programs had admitted female students, most of whom were religious, since the 1920s.

The open welcoming of women undergraduates was another matter, however. The impact on the Midtown campus was immediate, significant, and as Fr. Reinert remembers it, very positive. It started at the level of residential life. Although throughout the '40s and even into the '50s Saint Louis University was predominantly a commuter school, there were dormitories housing hundreds of students. Discipline in these male residence halls was strict by today's standards, but actual living conditions were, in the words of one who remembers, "a stinky zoo." The male students, away from home for the first time, did what young university men have done for centuries: they led raucous and sometimes rather unsanitary existences in dormitory rooms decorated with athletic trophies, liquor bottles, musical instruments, and other souvenirs. When women arrived on campus they were housed in women's dormitories, but they often took their meals with the male students and socialized with them constantly. The men, we are told, began to "clean up their act." Contemporary feminists of both genders may wince at the notion that women were what was then called a "civilizing influence" on the campus climate of the 1940s, but such appears to have been the case.

The first full-fledged women undergraduates at Saint Louis University were, of course, much more than simply a civilizing influence. They were from the start serious about their studies and about professional careers. Saint Louis University never offered a finishing school type education to the young women who sought admission to its programs. As an urban Jesuit institution, the University attracted women who were planning professional careers, most commonly in education, health care, and social work, and who came from similar socioeconomic backgrounds as their male counterparts. Like Saint Louis University's male students, most women undergraduates came from the St. Louis area and were graduates of the parochial schools.

Generally these women were welcomed by the male students and faculty, although a few unreconstructed Jesuit professors took a dim view of women undergraduates. One mathematics instructor grumbled that women could not do mathematics, "not even nuns." This relatively faint opposition was a reflection of the continuing gap, partially generational and partially cultural, which separated Jesuits on the question of women's education. Much of the European-dominated leadership of the Society of Jesus looked back to an earlier time when home and family were considered the only appropriate domains of women. Indeed, at the time when women were first entering through the front door as it were of Saint Louis University's undergraduate programs, many European nations had not yet given women the vote. Still, even the skeptics had to concede that women students kept the University, and in particular the College of Arts and Sciences, from floundering during the war years when the men were away at the war. Female students upheld and even raised the academic standards of the University while at the same time beginning the process of expansion and reinterpretation of the University to a broadening constituency which would continue in the postwar decades. The Women's Sodality was a major focus of social life and provided leadership training for the women. Many who were students at that time remember Fr. Benjamin Fulkerson, who was known as the "apostle to the women" and taught popular courses in marriage and counseling. The appointment of Nancy McNeir Ring as the first dean of women further confirmed the status of undergraduate women into the future.

During the Second World War women students became increasingly involved in student organizations, running the campus newspaper and the yearbook, among other activities. The situation changed somewhat when the war ended and a wave of determined and practically minded ex-G.I.s swamped the campus. After being the center of attention, women students now had to compete with men who wanted a degree in a hurry.

The first women faculty at the University were members of the Sisters of St. Mary who taught at the School of Nursing. The first female dean of the School of Nursing was Sister Mary Geraldine Kulleck, S.S.M., who served in this capacity from 1941 to 1953 and later as dean of the School of Nursing and Health Services from 1961 to 1966. Other prominent women on the faculty included Sister Mary Agnita Claire Day, who later served as dean, Sister Mary Dolorosa Pope at the Medical Center, and Sister Mary Imelda Pingel, Technology Department. Among the best remembered early female instructors in the School of Social Work were Dr. Katharine Radke, Ruth Joyce, Frieda Brackebusch, Marian DeVoy, and Virginia Ebbinghouse. Dr. Gladys Gruenberg, a professor of economics, was one of the first women to teach in the Business School. Other pioneers included Mrs. Jett Sullivan and Marjorie Moissner in the English department, Mrs. Esther Tillman in modern languages, and Mrs. Virginia Kern in mathematics.

African Americans

One of the most significant recurring themes in the history of the University over the past half century has been its relations with the African American community. As we have already seen, from the early decades of the century onward the Frost Campus has found itself in a racially diverse neighborhood. The initial reaction of the University to its non-white neighbors was to ignore them, but beginning in the 1940s it struck out in a new direction, seeking to place its resources at the disposal of its neighbors. It is, of course, far easier to express such sentiments than to put them into action. Once the decision was made to reach out to the African American community, serious questions needed to be answered: What were the needs of the community? What services should be offered to the community? In what form should these services be offered? Who best represented the interests of the community? What could the community bring to the University?

The initial decision to be the first educational institution in a former slave state to open its doors to black students occurred during the presidency of Fr. Patrick Holloran, and was in the difficult process of implementation when Fr. Reinert arrived at the University as dean of the College of Arts and Sciences in the summer of 1944. In the beginning Fr. Reinert was inspired and assisted by Fr. Claude H. Heithaus, assistant professor of classical archeology and a pioneer in integration efforts, Fr. George Dunne, a faculty member in the Institute for Social Order, and, in the outside community, the Jesuit Markoe brothers, who were leaders in pastoral work on behalf of the inner city African American community. With their guidance, Fr. Reinert was able to establish relationships with several ministers of black churches throughout the city, who in turn spread the word that the University now welcomed working together with the African American community. Whites and blacks began to meet together, but there were barriers on both sides that had to be overcome. The legacy of slavery and Jim Crow had left many African Americans distrustful of any white overtures, regardless of their stated intentions. On the University's side, there were naïve assumptions about what it would take to bring groups of people so long estranged together for a common purpose. Lack of contact between the races prevented white University administrators from realizing at first that they should not be the only ones setting the agenda and that African Americans were perfectly capable of articulating their own needs and desires and planning courses of action. At times some felt that the University came across as patronizing, but gradually progress was made.

In the midst of the upheavals and expansion which took place during World War II, and following on the discussion which had already begun regarding the admission of African Americans to the University, a sermon by Fr. Heithaus brought the issues to a head by bringing it to the attention of the students of the University. The sermon, preached on February 11, 1944, at the Saint Francis Xavier College Church, created a sensation. Eyewitnesses recall that Fr. Heithaus, a scholarly, bespectacled professor, spoke quietly and without dramatic flourishes:

It is a surprising and rather bewildering fact, that in what concerns justice for the Negro, the Mohammedans and the atheists are more Christ-like than many Christians. The followers of Mohammed and of Lenin make no distinction of color; but to some followers of Christ, the color of a man's skin makes all the difference in the world.

Our Lord and model, Jesus Christ, commanded His followers to teach all nations. He founded one church through which all were to be saved. He prayed that all might become one in Him. He incorporated all races and colors into His Mystical Body. He died that all might be united in happiness of the Beatific Vision.

Following in His footsteps, the Apostles taught these doctrines to all races and to all colors. One of their first converts was a Negro. But some people say that these doctrines do not apply to the Negro. If he is taught the religion and morality of Christ, it must be under conditions that are humiliating or financially impossible. . . .

Now some people say that if the Society of Jesus gives Catholic Negroes the Catholic education which the Church wishes them to have, our White students will walk out on us. Is this true? I deny it. I say it is a lie and a libel. I challenge the whole world to prove that even one of our Catholic students will desert us when we apply the principles for which Jesus Christ suffered and died. . . .

. . . Do you want us to slam our doors in the face of Catholics, because their complexion happens to be brown or black?

It is a lie. I see that you repudiate it with indignation. You scorn it all the more because you know that some of the very people who disseminate this lie have themselves sent their sons to Harvard and Yale, where they were glad to sit in the same classrooms with Negroes. Those people bow in

reverence before Oxford and Cambridge, the University of
London and Sorbonne, but if they ever attended these great
Universities, as I have, they would soon learn that in the
world of scholarship there is neither White nor Black, Brown
nor Yellow. . . .

Fr. Heithaus went on to describe what, from his perspective, was the
greatest danger posed by race prejudice to the world, the Catholic
Church, and its people:

Your responsibility is very great, so great that it almost
frightens me. Do you realize that if the Negroes are snubbed
by the followers of Christ, they will turn in despair to the
followers of Lenin? Do you realize that Communist
agitators, specially trained at Moscow, have already made
more than a hundred thousand converts among them, and are
pouring out the vials of their wrath upon the Catholic
Church, accusing it of being indifferent to the wrongs of the
Negro?

Who can fight this fire of hatred and indignation against
Christ and His church? Who can stop it from becoming a
conflagration that will consume us all? Only Catholics can
do it. Catholic leaders, White and Black, thoroughly
grounded in Catholic principles and trained in Catholic
universities, where the doctrine of the Mystical Body of
Christ is taught and practiced, and there is neither White nor
Black, but all Christians are equal in Christ Jesus.[1]

There are several interesting details to the story of Fr. Heithaus's
sermon which have never been told. The first concerns how the sermon
itself reached the campus community and the rest of St. Louis.
According to Mary Bruemmer, who was later dean of women at the
University, Fr. Heithaus inserted the text of the sermon into the
University News the night before he delivered it, placing the editor's

---

[1] Jack Maguire, "Race Prejudice Denounced: Jesuit Says Christ's Teaching Must
Prevail," *The University News*, 11 February, 1944.

name, Jack Maguire, on the article. As a result, within a few hours after it was delivered, the sermon was read by hundreds of students and was picked up by the *Globe-Democrat* and the *Post-Dispatch*, which gave it considerable publicity. Even more noteworthy than the way the sermon was disseminated was its original audience. Since Fr. Heithaus spoke to a wartime student body, the overwhelming majority of students attending Mass that Friday morning were women. The enthusiasm and support of these and other women for the call for integration was instrumental in bringing about this change. These women identified with the struggle African Americans were undertaking to receive an education, having begun their own struggle not so many years before.

From our perspective more than half a century later, it may be a little difficult to grasp how radical Fr. Heithaus's words were. Not only was St. Louis a segregated city where slavery had flourished within the memory of people still living, but the Missouri Province of the Society of Jesus, whose southern boundaries reached to the Louisiana state line, had members with strong ties to the South who still bore scars from the Civil War of eighty years before. High-ranking Jesuits, such as the Very Reverend Joseph Zuercher, favored a gradual approach at best to racial integration, while many Catholics felt it would be better to "leave well enough alone." But Fr. Heithaus's sermon and the subsequent explosion of debate at the University put the issues of integration squarely before the student body, who were called upon to renounce racism and strive for racial justice. It would be pleasant to report that the entire University community, including its spiritual leaders, rallied behind Fr. Heithaus once he had taken the step of placing the issue of racial discrimination squarely in front of the University community, and by implication, the entire city. This, however, was not the case. While many faculty and students enthusiastically supported his call to repudiate racism in the name of the Gospel, others took a much dimmer view of Fr. Heithaus's sermon. President Holloran was angered and offended by the unexpected call for acceptance of non-whites. It is not clear whether Fr. Holloran was motivated chiefly by fears of how parents and alumni would react to the prospect of an integrated University, or whether he actually believed that African Americans did not belong at Saint Louis University because of their alleged intellectual or moral inferiority. What is evident is that concern over parental reactions was made the principal argument against the integration of the

University. President Holloran also claimed, but without evidence, that students attending the sermon had felt intimidated into responding to Heithaus's call to abandon racism. Fr. Holloran's concerns were echoed and amplified by those of then-Archbishop Glennon, a powerful force in the community. In the words of one writer, ". . . the controversy brought out the darker side of some otherwise good men. . . . Glennon was angered by the Heithaus sermon and vented his displeasure in a face to face confrontation with the Jesuit."[2]

After a half hour of dressing down by Archbishop Glennon, Heithaus was compelled to spend three days in seclusion, praying and doing penance. He was also the subject of a "chapter," a disciplinary procedure in the Society of Jesus in which a miscreant is formally and publicly reprimanded. Shortly thereafter, the archeology professor "chose" to be transferred to Marquette University, where he remained for several years. Afterwards he returned to St. Louis, where he maintained a distinctly low profile for the rest of his career. In the meantime, on April 25, 1944, Holloran having apparently reconsidered, announced that the University had an obligation to provide a Catholic education to all people, regardless of color, and that summer session the first five African American students were enrolled. Fr. Claude Heithaus died on May 12, 1976, having lived to see the transformation he sparked draw hundreds of people of color to the University's programs, but without receiving just recognition for his contribution to the development of the University.

After Fr. Holloran's announcement, the University placed advertisements in local newspapers saying that it was now admitting African Americans. One African American who responded was Sylvester L. Smith, who, with four other African Americans, enrolled that summer of 1944. At the time he was a teacher who needed further course work in order to receive his permanent superintendent certificate. Smith completed his master's degree in the University's department of education in 1947. Anita Lyons Bond, a fifteen-year-old African American girl who had graduated from her high school in just three years, enrolled as an undergraduate in 1946. She spent four years at the University, graduated with honors, and was the first African American to be admitted into the national Jesuit honor society, now

---

[2] Daniel J. Ladd, "History Lessons," *Universitas* (Spring 1995), p. 16.

known as Alpha Sigma Nu.

These and other African American pioneers had to balance their lives between the relatively tolerant atmosphere of the University and the continuing discrimination of the surrounding society which infringed daily on their experiences. Saint Louis University, lacking at the time a dining hall, contracted with a local cafe to provide student meals. Since this cafe would not serve African Americans, these students had to bring their own lunches from home. On another occasion, the Chase Park Plaza Hotel was the setting for a reception for students and their families. Although the hotel had a policy of not serving "colored people," the University insisted that all students would have to be served at University functions, and the hotel complied.

The University can look back with pride to these and other instances of its standing up to discriminatory practices, but those who led the fight to end discrimination are quick to add that the battle is still far from over. Legal segregation has ended, but equality of educational opportunity at the pre-university level has not yet been achieved. Economic inequality continues to have a profound impact on the educational experiences of African Americans.

Among the many distinguished African American graduates of Saint Louis University in the years which followed its integration, one of the most prominent educators is Dr. Cal Burnett. While an undergraduate at the University in the late 1950s, Burnett played collegiate varsity basketball at a time when many teams, particularly in the South, had only white players. During a four-team holiday tournament at Tulane University in New Orleans, Burnett found himself barred from the basketball courts because of a Louisiana state law prohibiting state schools from competing against teams with African American players. Fr. Reinert, when informed of this, responded by saying that if Burnett could not play, the entire team would stay home. Within two days, two more teams in the tournament, Notre Dame and the University of Dayton, also withdrew, leaving Tulane without a tournament to host.

On another occasion, the Billikens were playing at North Texas State, in Denton, Texas, when a hotel clerk refused to give Burnett a room because of his color. Burnett remembers vividly what followed: "I went up and said, 'If I don't have a room in five minutes, call Fr. Reinert, reverse the charges, and tell him of the trouble. You know what will happen then!' I had a room in three minutes." Experiences such as these reminded University faculty and students that while their school was integrated without incident, the rest of the world was often different. In Missouri itself, the last law supporting segregation of public school children by race was not taken off the books until 1977.

The University's approach to the complex problems of race relations evolved over time into a multi-faceted attack. First, programs were developed to make it possible for persons of color to take advantage of the resources of the University. In concrete terms this meant establishing financial aid and academic support programs, and actively recruiting non-Caucasian students. While Fr. Reinert was and remains emphatically opposed to the notion of racial quotas, he recognized that a passive approach to integration would bring few non-white students to campus, and that the most able members of minority groups would have to be actively sought out. Another component to the drive to make the campus available to what would later be called "non-traditional" students was the founding of Metropolitan College in September 1962. Metropolitan College, which existed until the fall of 1990, was created as an evening school offering both certificate programs and college credit classes at a greatly reduced tuition. While Metropolitan College did not explicitly target African Americans, the College did strive to bring members of the neighboring communities onto campus, where, in many cases, they received a taste of college life which ultimately led to the pursuit of a degree. Metropolitan College, which was subsidized by the University, was eventually phased out, not because of any failure in delivering education to the community, but because the region's community colleges, its natural competition, were less expensive, and in many cases more conveniently located.

The University continues to provide special opportunities to all students who may enter it with various disadvantages. One of its more recent programs is the Med Prep program, in which every year 10 to 20 students are admitted for special instruction in the basic science courses prior to formal admission to the Medical School. Although when this program was developed a decade ago some members of the Medical School faculty objected strenuously, over two-thirds of the students entering the program have been admitted to the Medical School and have graduated with an M.D. degree.

During the Vietnam War era in the late '60s and early '70s, Saint Louis University did not experience the widespread violent upheavals which paralyzed campuses across the country. Observers credited the conservative Catholic school background of the undergraduates, the basically conservative nature of the city of St. Louis, and the productive contacts between students and the Board of Trustees for the relatively calm mood on campus during this time. There were moments, however, where the focus of the overwhelmingly white student body seemed to collide with the concerns of African American students. On one occasion a huge concourse of students gathered to protest the presence on campus of an ROTC office in Choteau House (now known as Cupples House). Subsequently, an even larger crowd assembled in Busch Center to press their demands against ROTC when a small contingent of African American students entered the room, marched to the podium, seized the microphone from Fr. Reinert, who had been addressing the crowd, and told the crowd that its passion and concerns were misplaced. They said that while students were rallying to protest the consequences of a war being fought thousands of miles away, they were ignoring the needs of those who lived around them. The African American student representatives presented a list of grievances to which Fr. Reinert attempted to respond. He never forgot how the white students' impatient, even hostile mood toward the administration dramatically changed to an attitude defending the University in the face of criticism from the African American students. What began as a protest meeting against the University administration ended with the African American students exiting from a room where the hostility was directed toward them.

Any institution which claims to be committed to the idea of racial integration must do more than simply try to recruit students from different backgrounds. It must have a racially diverse governing body. Fr. Reinert and Board Chairman Dan Schlafly therefore resolved to incorporate a second component in their strategy to bringing the University closer to the African American community. Together they approached Roy Wilkins, head of the NAACP in New York City, to serve on the Board of Trustees. Wilkins first discussed all the possible reasons why he might not be the best choice, but ultimately accepted and became the first nonwhite member of the Board of a Catholic college or university. Wilkins, who served on the board from 1967 to 1976, focused much of his efforts on the Trustee Committee for Student Life, where the social integration and the self-image of African students were major concerns.

A recent series of celebrations commemorating "Fifty Years of Integration at Saint Louis University" produced tangible evidence of the unique pioneering contributions that the University has made toward raising the educational and economic level of African Americans in metropolitan St. Louis. Highlights of the 50th anniversary commemoration included:

- A lecture in the College Church by Andrew Young, internationally known civil and human rights leader, who praised the capacity integrated audience of faculty and students for "reaffirming the faith of their predecessors who risked integration fifty years ago."

- A PBS Teleconference in which students, faculty, staff, and administration reviewed the University's culture of diversity and inclusiveness, describing community building as the "ultimate liberal art!"

- A forum featuring African American alumni and alumnae from the '70s, '80s, and '90s who shared their own personal student-life experiences and subsequent career achievements.

All materials from this year-long celebration were buried in a time capsule outside Busch Memorial Center, to be opened in the year 2044, the 100th anniversary of racial integration at Saint Louis University.

It is important to point out here that the University's early and courageous decision to offer equal educational opportunities to minority students was in fact just one application of the unique aspect of Jesuit higher educational philosophy which calls for preferential concern for the poor and deprived in every category of human disability. Beyond the particularly striking example of early integration, the University continues to distinguish itself in several other areas of services on behalf of the poor and/or deprived. For example, through the Disabilities Coordinator's office and the Affirmative Action Office students with academic or physical disabilities are helped to develop study skills and learning strategies aimed at enabling them to achieve sufficient independence to become successful students. A wide variety of the most modern technical equipment is provided to empower students with various challenges to achieve academic success at the University.

And nowhere is the University's commitment to a compassionate philosophy of "equal opportunity" more evident than the long-standing record of financial aid which compares most impressively with similar programs in other colleges and universities across the country. Both the variety of scholarships as well as the amount of financial assistance has grown annually to a record total of $20 million being awarded to 4,188 students in the 1994–95 academic year. A small sampling of the amazing variety of funded programs:

- Presidential, Dean, and University Tuition/Dorm Scholarships awarded for academic achievement;

- Ignatian Service and Volunteer Leadership Tuition/Dorm grants;

- Calloway/Wilkins Scholarships awarded to African Americans for academic and leadership qualities.

This chapter has attempted to describe the dramatic changes which have been taking place in American higher education, specifically at Saint Louis University. We chose the dramatic changes in women's education and the pioneering admission and integration of African Americans as most illustrative of the changes at Saint Louis University. But obviously there were many other changes taking place in all of American society such as the invasion of "world culture," changing moral standards and perspectives, etc., all of which has had a substantial impact on Saint Louis University. The following chapters will attempt to describe the changes which took place inside the University, e.g., governance structure, as we tried to keep ahead of, or at least to keep up with, the unyielding demands for change created by an American society which seems ill-prepared to enter the twenty-first century.

CHAPTER
THREE

THE THREE
ESSENTIALS

*AN ARMY OF STAGS LED BY A LION WOULD BE BETTER THAN AN
ARMY OF LIONS LED BY A STAG.*

—LATIN PROVERB

Although a simplified definition of the multiple tasks of the president of a major university is obviously open to questioning in today's complicated society, it still can be argued that a successful university president must divide his or her time among three essential aspects of the job: academic leadership, internal administration, and friend-and-fund-raising. Each of these components makes different demands on a university president's time and energies, and each administrator will feel more or less comfortable with the carrying out of the different components, although administrators too often do not feel well-trained in all three. Moreover, at various points in the governance of the university the urgent demands

29

of one component can overshadow the needs of others. Nevertheless, all three must be attended to for the university to function well. Because of the limited time and attention a university president can devote to each of these three essential duties, it is imperative that the president have highly qualified vice presidents who serve specifically as his or her representative in each of these three categories. Hence, the vice president for academics, the vice president for finance and the vice president for institutional advancement (public relations and development) are absolutely essential members of the president's "team"—but the too common defect in such an arrangement lies in the temptation on the part of the president to delegate too much responsibility in one or another of these essential areas without insisting on frequent consultation and joint decision-making. In fact, university administration today is so complex and demanding that a president can keep abreast of developments in each of these three essential areas only with an "alter ego"(sometimes called a provost), an experienced, broad-gauged, extremely competent administrator who shares the president's authority and responsibilities. During Fr. Reinert's long regime as president, Fr. Jerome J. Marchetti, S.J., carried out these functions extremely well as executive vice president. We will now consider some of the implications of carrying out each of these three essentials.

ACADEMIC LEADERSHIP

Administrators, faculty, and students will agree that the role of the university president has become far less personal as this century has progressed. A hundred years ago, even such an august figure as Harvard's president, Charles W. Eliot, handled much of his correspondence himself, and met with prospective students and their families on a regular basis. At Saint Louis University, as at many Jesuit schools, the personal style and work schedule of the president was for many years an easily recognizable feature of campus life. The president was more than an administrator; he was a discernible personality whose strengths and foibles shaped the learning climate. The personal influence of the school's chief executive, whether it was perceived as benign or intrusive, formed an important part of what historian Frederick Rudolph has called the "college way," a conception of higher education as a highly personal, joint undertaking possessing many of the characteristics of a family.

The modern American university, be it Catholic or not, has found it very difficult to perpetuate this tradition. The size, specialization, and physical fragmentation of the modern university have contributed to this. Moreover, the pressures and responsibilities that have been outlined in previous chapters, as well as the evolving role of the university president, have led many presidents away from their earlier interactions with students and faculty. While the reasons for this shift are understandable, the negative consequences of the isolation of the university president from both direct and indirect contact with students are profound. Students, consciously or unconsciously, recognize and tend to value those things that the university calls attention to and elevates. If students arrive at the conclusion that the administration, as personified by the university president, does not pay attention to them and therefore does not value them, their own attitudes toward their education and personal development will suffer. The president of a Jesuit institution, both as a symbol of the institution and as a highly visible representative of the spiritual tradition that the university espouses, is in a unique position to influence students. This does not mean that the president must clear his daily calendar of administrative and community-related matters in order to embark on a string of undergraduate cookouts and pizza parties, but it does mean that he must cultivate a climate of accessibility, openness, and, to an extent, visibility. Something as simple as regularly being seen walking across campus or turning up periodically in the dining halls to sample the cuisine can begin to make a difference, not merely in the president's personal popularity, but in the sense of community and caring which prevails on campus. There are, of course, more substantive things the president and other administrators can do to promote a sense of inclusion and community. For many years Saint Louis University maintained a Student Leadership Council made up of undergraduates but unrelated to Student Government, which met with the president and was able to convey student concerns on a less formal basis. There are many other venues in which the university president can encounter students in a credible fashion. Work with student volunteer groups and with special interest groups allows both administrator and students to meet in a nonadversarial setting which goes beyond the boisterous bonhomie of a football game. In each instance, it is the quality, not the quantity, of the encounter that makes the difference.

At the same time it is worth noting how much of what works for students also is applicable to faculty. Most faculty do not demand much explicitly from their president; many faculty view administrators as a necessary evil and hope merely to be left alone by them. Yet faculty, too, react to what the university makes clear in its agenda. Faculty, too, look for leadership, and for a sense that their leader understands and values what they are about. At a Catholic university, there is need for a president who can maintain the balance between upholding the Catholic traditions of the institution and responding to the diverse communities both within and outside the university. This job has never been easy, and despite the relative calm of American university campuses, is harder than ever today. Increasingly, both Catholic university students and faculty are not products of traditional Catholic education. This in itself need not be an insurmountable problem (and in a later chapter we will propose a way to perpetuate Jesuit values among lay faculty), but it means that the administrator must educate not only the surrounding community as to the mission of the university, but on occasion the university faculty as well. Formal lectures and periodic appearances at faculty functions are a small part, at best, of this role. Much more important is the president's ability to project a persona that commands the intellectual respect of the faculty along with credibility as the spokesperson for the preservation of basic Christian values in the midst of ongoing dynamic change. This is a much harder assignment than even the admittedly difficult job of heading a non-church affiliated school. Catholic university presidents in the next century will not be able to dodge controversy, much as they might like to. Many of these controversies are identical with those their lay colleagues grapple with: faculty grievances related to tenure, debates about the "political correctness" of this or that course, demands from various advocacy groups, and complaints from skeptical alumni about all of the above. But the Catholic university president must also lead an institution which is simultaneously aligned with a world Church and, as some see it, an American Catholic Church, as well as being an institution whose mission is tied to American culture. This means that the university is inevitably influenced by cultural trends and social developments in that culture. In particular, the struggle between the universal claims of the Church and the push for cultural and geographical autonomy within the Church which will certainly continue for a long time into the future place the Catholic university, and especially its president, in the unenviable spotlight of publicity. When a university administrator, for example, claims to uphold academic freedom, while defending the traditional teachings of the Church, some may call the performance ingenuous, insincere, or worse. Yet the roles of president as spokesperson for a Church-affiliated institution and representative of a liberal intellectual tradition can never be completely separated, and every pronouncement made by a university president is liable to be placed in both contexts by friends and foes alike.

It may sound simplistic, but in the end the success which an administrator experiences can have less to do with knowledge of canon law, trends in sociology, or medical ethics, than with the perceived character of the leader of the university community. "Perceived" is of key importance here; university faculty members, despite their reputation for being sometimes fractious and cynical, will give a great deal of credit to a president whom they perceive as principled, organized, and in possession of a vision for the future, even if that vision is not entirely identical with their own. Disagreements between administrators and faculty are inevitable, but what often brings university presidents to grief is not a difference of opinion, but the suspicion that they are not dealing candidly with the problem at hand or that they lack the skill or courage to do the right thing, or to inspire others to do likewise.

If a university president can manage, through inspiration, grace, force of character, vision, and yes, occasional luck, to gain the necessary confidence of the students and faculty in order to be the academic leader, only the first phase of the job is completed. The actual day-to-day managing of the university remains.

INTERNAL FISCAL AND MANAGERIAL ADMINISTRATION

Up until the mid-1900s, the second of the three essential responsibilities of a university president—fiscal management—was probably the most frightening task, especially in a Catholic institution in which typically the priest or nun in charge rarely had experience and/or training in financial matters. Up until Fr. Reinert's tenure, the Jesuits at Saint Louis University had been fortunate in identifying among their associates a number of Jesuits who were "late vocations," men who had had years of experience as business managers, accountants, etc., before their decision to enter religious life. But in view of the fact that the vast majority of young Jesuits were entering immediately out of high school,

Fr. Reinert early on decided to seek experienced laymen from the business community to manage the various aspects of the financial assets of the University: construction and control, investments of a growing endowment, building and real estate management, insurance and risk management, computerization, etc. Early lay fiscal managers, assisted by experienced business leaders on the Finance Committee of the Board of Trustees, gradually brought the business office in line with the standards developed by the National Association of College and University Business Officers (NACUBO). Several early lay pioneers come to mind: Fred Bertram, wooed away from Stix, Baer & Fuller by Fr. Reinert to become the University's first lay chief financial officer; Edwin Lanwerth, who succeeded Bertram; Ed Hellman, first layman to carry the title of financial vice president, and John Fox, who had retired as a very successful president of Mercantile Bank and Trust, and who was especially skilled in the area of real estate and investments, both of which represented growth areas in the University's financial structure.

If any evidence were needed to prove how essentially important to the University's stability and continuity was the establishment of a Board of Trustees with a key committee of experienced business persons concentrating on University finances, one needs only to review the all-University annual financial reports and audits to understand how the University has gone from antiquated budgetary processes to highly sophisticated financial planning and controls. Immensely impressive as is the current replacement value of $482 million of our buildings and grounds (comprising 150 acres of land: Frost campus, 100 acres, and Health Sciences Center, 50) as well as our 1994–95 operating budget of $515 million, far more significant for the University's future is the current evaluation of University endowment at its highest level of $402 million—a gigantic leap from the only $2 million, mostly earmarked for the School of Medicine, of fifty years ago.

INSTITUTIONAL ADVANCEMENT AND FUND-RAISING

Of the three essential tasks incumbent in a private university president, guaranteeing academic quality and integrity, overseeing a sound financial management system, and building a sophisticated program for attracting the immediate and long-range financial support necessary for healthy growth, Fr. Reinert soon became convinced that the last—institutional advancement, i.e., fund-raising— called for his greatest efforts. However, the necessary ingredients for embarking on a sound fund-raising program first had to be assembled.

Like all Jesuit institutions of higher education in the 1950s, Saint Louis University was governed by an all-Jesuit Board of Trustees. The Board was made up of six key administrators, such as the president and the financial vice president or procurator as he was then called, and exercised virtually total control over the long-range fate of the institution. Hence the governing as well as the financial well-being of the University was seen to be the special responsibility of representatives of the Jesuit community. Earlier Jesuit presidents had sporadically called upon business leaders and wealthy friends to support the University. Fr. Robert S. Johnston, who had been president in the 1930s, had compiled a list of local business people, a few of them alumni, who had been approached for contributions. The list detailed who had contributed and who had not. Contributions, by late twentieth-century standards, were small. The Depression and the demands of a wartime economy further limited the scale of contributions, as did the backgrounds and careers of many Saint Louis university graduates of the '20s, '30s, and '40s. Like other urban Catholic universities and colleges of its day, Saint Louis University served as a stepping stone to the middleclass i.e., for the children of frequently struggling immigrant parents. Once graduates left Saint Louis University, many felt that they had already "paid their dues" to the institution, and in any case few graduates had become wealthy enough to become big donors to their alma mater. Unlike some previously small and relatively unknown universities such as Notre Dame or Fordham, Saint Louis University had not embarked on a program of institutional self-promotion through collegiate football, nor had a Carnegie or Rockefeller taken an interest in the Jesuit university. As late as the 1940s, most administrators took the attitude that Saint Louis University could survive almost from hand-to-mouth on tuition and on the occasional modest windfall that came its way. Fr. Pat Holloran, Fr. Reinert's immediate predecessor, was the first to launch a loosely organized campaign with the help of local Catholic business leaders such as Leo Wieck, Frank Guyol, Harry Harrington, and Andy Mungenast. He also brought in Joe Maniaci of Fordham football fame to launch a football program that would challenge that of the University of Notre Dame.

But in the meantime the University struggled to overcome serious obstacles to sound growth: a modest endowment mostly designated for the Medical School, a "street car" campus geared mostly for commuters, with underdeveloped physical facilities and scientific equipment. Yet this underdeveloped situation in no way could be attributed to deficiencies on the part of administrators and staff of the university.

Rather, during much of the first century of its operation, and especially after the "Know Nothing" conflicts of the ante-bellum era, Saint Louis University had been forced to be an inward-looking institution. While this inward focus allowed the University to develop academic programs which produced numerous distinguished prelates, scholars, and even community leaders, there was also a high price to be paid for the decades of isolation which grew up between the University and the immediate outside world. By the early decades of this century Washington University, a newer institution, had far outstripped Saint Louis University in wealth and in visibility in the community. The sons of prominent turn-of-the-century St. Louis Catholics and Protestants alike attended "Wash. U.," while their fathers supported the university's growing endowment. Among the men vowed to religious poverty and committed to making educational opportunity available to those who needed it the most, not surprisingly an attitude prevailed at most Catholic schools of the period that expenses could and should be met in large part by tuition, and that there was no need to devote time and energy to the building up of generous endowments. Many university teachers and administrators, moreover, viewed fund-raising as a "dirty business" typical of a money-grubbing world which they had chosen to avoid or rise above. This philosophy, reinforced by the missionary origins of many of this country's Catholic schools, contrasted with the tendency of other private colleges and universities to amass endowments that by the 1920s sometimes were in the tens of millions of dollars. The hardships of the Depression and the decline in enrollment during World War II further delayed the development of a sizable endowment for the University.

When Fr. Reinert succeeded Fr. Holloran as University president in 1949, he quickly adopted a philosophy which acknowledged that fund-raising must be an essential part of any university's activities and, therefore, an important facet of a university president's responsibilities. As indicated earlier, Fr. Reinert described his conception of a university president as being one-third academic leader, one-third internal administrator, and one-third fund-raiser. He recognized, however, that fund-raising was a more complex undertaking than simply approaching wealthy individuals and corporations for donations. The University must educate the entire business community as to what it was and did. Just as important as finding a donor was locating those individuals in the business and civic community who could act as spokespersons and protagonists for the University. To initiate such a program of area-wide cultivation, recognition and moral support, William Durbin was appointed the University's first vice president for Public Relations. Bill went on to become CEO of Hill and Knowlton in New York City, at that time the largest public relations firm in this country.

Fortunately, a forum for Saint Louis University exposure was found in Civic Progress, an organization of the heads of leading business concerns in the St. Louis area. The greatest asset of this organization, its tight-knit composition of leading business figures, might also be seen as its most significant liability, for while Civic Progress had the power to make things happen, it did not include among its members organized labor, minorities, or women. Nevertheless, Civic Progress was still of value to the University since it counted as ex officio members the chief executives of Washington University and Saint Louis University, and so Fr. Reinert immediately had access to the groups who could furnish the University with its spokesman for his first fund-raising effort called the Priority Needs campaign, a drive that had as its goal the raising of $18 million. Fr. Reinert set his sights still higher. Against the advice of his "kitchen cabinet," the president decided to approach August (Gussie) Busch, Jr., head of the Anheuser-Busch Brewing Company. Some felt that Busch, a noted man-about-town who had never attended college, was too rough-hewn and lacked sufficient experience with education to be an effective representative of the University's interests. Busch himself was convinced that he had no talent as a speaker. Fr. Reinert persisted, offering the brewing magnate lessons from the University's Speech Department and scripts written by University personnel. With considerable reluctance, Busch agreed to become the chairman of the Priority Needs campaign. There followed a transformation in the life of August Busch worthy of a tale by Charles Dickens. Busch gave addresses to his business colleagues, hosted gala events at his famous suburban estate, Grant's Farm, and made generous donations to the University. Over time, he discovered that the students to whom he gave scholarships were truly grateful for the assistance, and that the directors of University projects which he sponsored acknowledged his contributions. According to those who knew him well, he evolved from a businessman with no direct interest in higher education to an alumni father who sent five of his children to Saint Louis University. The most visible contributions to the University from Gussie, and his son August III, are the Busch Memorial Center, the Anheuser-Busch wing of Pius XII Library, and the Anheuser-Busch Eye Institute. The children of Gussie created a Scholarship Endowment Fund totaling nearly $1,000,000 in his memory. And subsequently Gertrude (Trudy) Buholzer Busch established an even larger trust to provide scholarships, especially for students in the School of Nursing, from which her daughter Trudy Busch Valentine graduated in 1980.

Saint Louis University found other ways to reach the city's commercial and industrial leaders. One way was to educate them about the already existing impact which the University had on the business work force. Thousands of graduates of the University's business programs worked in the St. Louis area, far outnumbering the graduates of Washington University, large numbers of whom left Missouri after graduation. By stressing the practical benefits of employing University graduates, Fr. Reinert sought to persuade local businesses that financial support for the University was an investment in their own future.

At the same time, Fr. Reinert realized that the University's own graduates were an untapped source of support. He asked Fr. Francis O'Reilly, S.J., a professor of philosophy and a dynamic personality, to head the University's first annual alumni fund. O'Reilly and Fr. Reinert's original technique was to ask alumni to become the University's "Living Endowment" by providing a pool of funds to increase faculty salaries. Fund-raising drives also pitted graduates of different Schools against one another in a friendly competition that raised money and fostered a sense of identity and loyalty among graduates. Emphasized from the beginning was accountability on the part of the University—reporting to donors the designation and results of their giving as a major incentive for continuing support. For example, donors of money for scholarships were informed of the names of student recipients and their academic progress, as well as an opportunity to meet these students if so desired. Ironically, both the growing close relationship of the University to business leaders and the inclusion of non-Catholics in the life of the University were reminiscent of the 1820s and 1830s, when the fledgling school and the frontier community had worked closely together and Protestants had sent their sons to be educated by the Jesuits.

Saint Louis University has in recent decades been very successful in raising funds. Today the endowment of the University has reached $402 million, of which over $170 million has been raised since 1989. This remarkable achievement and the planning of future fund-raising programs has been the result not only of efforts of the current University president, Fr. Lawrence Biondi, but of the professional approach and sophisticated know-how of many Advancement officers such as Fr. J. Barry McGannon, S.J. Ultimately, though, the success of fund-raising depends in large part on the attention and focus which the president gives to it, and his collaboration with the Trustees Development Committee and the fund-raising and public relations staff. Moreover, the business of fund-raising is not only one of the most time-consuming responsibilities of a university president, but one that requires flexibility, humility, patience, and a sense of humor. Fr. Reinert's experiences in this field were at times demanding and even frustrating, but in the end more gratifying than he could have imagined.

Fund-Raising as a Ministry

Not only was there an emphasis on a systematic, professional approach to the essential task of securing financial support for the university, but Fr. Reinert strove to place this entire process in the context of a ministry. Just as there is a unique orientation which the mission of Saint Louis university offers to academic administrators, faculty, staff, and students, so there was special concern to impregnate the fund- and friend-raising personnel with a similar dedication to the same mission. In his own life and in his writings and speeches, Fr. Reinert has insisted "in season and out of season" that fund-raising is a ministry and that those who work to win friends and monetary support for the university are mightily involved in promoting the university's mission.

Unfortunately, as we have noted, many people tend to consider fund-raising a worldly preoccupation, even "dirty business," and at best look on it as bringing two seeming incompatibles—Christian life and values, and money-seeking—into an uneasy coalition. Yet the fact is that anyone, including a vowed religious, who engages in any aspect of development, can be carrying out a genuine Christian ministry, a ministry that should bring spiritual rewards equal to or surpassing the rewards of any other ministry, a ministry that should be respected and appreciated by superiors and other members of the community.

Fund-raising and development are dependent on a human phenomenon called philanthropy, literally, "love for mankind or human- kind, love for all human beings." The love we should have for all of our fellow men and women is fundamentally a spiritual concept. As a matter of fact, this concept of universal love is precisely the sole criterion that Jesus explicitly established for judging the success of a human life. "What you do or don't do to and for others, especially those who need it most, you do or don't do to and for me." Because of the identification of himself with the needy, philanthropy in the broad sense, i.e., universal unselfish love of our fellow human beings, becomes the essential indispensable evidence of our love of God.

A careful analysis of the process of fund-raising reveals that there are three categories of persons involved in philanthropy, all of whom ideally should partake in the spiritual motivations and benefits of the process: (1) the fund-raiser, the instigator or motivator of the process; (2) the donor; and (3) the beneficiary. It is a revolving process, personal and interpersonal, a continuing interaction among these three persons.

Necessary Spiritual Qualities in the Fund-Raiser

Over forty years of rubbing shoulders with all kinds of men and women engaged professionally in fund-raising, some as professional counselors, some in development departments of institutions and agencies, some working on their own, has revealed the wide variety of character traits which one finds in every profession. Over this long period of years some have achieved remarkable success, others created a flash-in-the-pan record only to disappear, others floated from one job to another with mediocrity, and still others leave the fund-raising field after a very short time to do something quite different. During that long period of observation of other fund-raisers combined with a matured self-knowledge of his own career, Fr. Reinert has tried to analyze the most important differences between the successful and unsuccessful fund-raising careers he has observed. Although the list could be much longer, four spiritual qualities have been substantially present and intermingled in the successful fund-raisers he has known.

First, commitment belongs at the top of the list: commitment to the cause and especially to the people the cause represents, to the job to be done, to volunteer workers, to the benefactors themselves. John Gardner says, "People can achieve meaning in their lives only if they have made commitments beyond the self-religious commitments, commitments to loved ones, to one's fellow humans, to excellence, to some conception of an ethical order—you give life meaning through your commitments." This is pre-eminently true in fund-raisers, who must commit their time and effort and total devotion. Any fund-raiser can put all there is to say about an institution or agency that needs and deserves help in an impressive video presentation, but what can never be put in pictures or in a brochure is one's own deep-down personal commitment to the cause.

Deep personal commitment carries with it the second inseparable companion quality: a genuine enthusiasm, not showmanship, that comes from an abiding feeling of privilege in having the joy of perpetuating and enhancing something that is destined to improve the quality of human lives. St. Paul says that God loves a cheerful giver; one might add that God also loves a cheerful fund-raiser.

Unselfishness, the third quality, always accompanies commitment and enthusiasm in any truly successful fund-raiser. A fund-raiser who is honestly committed to the cause does not care who receives the credit and kudos for getting the job done. Self-aggrandizement in a fund-raiser eventually alienates either the donors, his employers, or the community.

Finally, few vocations or professional careers demand deeper humility or longer lasting resilience than does development and fund-raising. Asking for money from someone whose wealth has made him rather arrogant or cynical is frequently a heroic act. Like a parent punishing a child, you will often have to say inwardly, "this hurts me more than it does you." There are people coarse enough to try to make you crawl if you ask them for some form of help. No one likes to be turned down, especially for a bogus reason.

These four inseparable qualities—commitment, enthusiasm, unselfishness, and resilient humility—constitute the spiritual essence of philanthropy in the fund-raiser. Ideally, his or her work should take on the characteristic of a ministry, the same kind of ministry, for example, that characterizes the leaders in the early Christian church. For example, it seems clear that the Apostle Paul considered fund-raising a legitimate and important function of his apostolic efforts to forward the Kingdom of Christ. Boldly, he tells his flock that as a minister of the Gospel, he must tell them not only to be aware of the needs of others but to do something about it. In reminding the Corinthians that their brethren in Jerusalem need their help, he ties his appeal for money directly to their moral, spiritual obligation: "The point is this: the one who sows sparingly will also reap sparingly, and the one who sows bountifully will also reap bountifully. Each of you must give as you have made up your mind, not reluctantly or under compulsion, for God loves a cheerful giver. " (2 Cor 9:6–7).[1]

Paul himself begs as part of his apostolate; he requires and praises the same in his apostolic followers. As he encourages his different flocks to vie with each other in generosity, he insists that those coming to them for this purpose do so in a spiritual capacity:

> We want you to know, brothers and sisters, about the grace of God that has been granted to the churches of Macedonia; for during a severe ordeal of affliction, their abundant joy and their extreme poverty have overflowed in a wealth of generosity on their part. For, as I can testify, they voluntarily gave according to their means, and even beyond their means, begging us earnestly for the privilege of sharing in this ministry to the saints—. . . so that might urge Titus that, as he had already made a beginning, so he should also complete this generous undertaking among you. (2 Cor 8:1–4. 6).

SPIRITUAL QUALITIES IN THE DONOR

Why do people give? What motivates a non-donor to become a cheerful giver? Research studies confirmed by Fr. Reinert's own experiences indicate that there are four key factors influencing individuals to give:

1. Personal need: giving presents an opportunity for an individual to actualize his/her best self-image.

2. Personal involvement: major gifts usually come from those who have become personally involved in the program.

3. Example of others: givers, especially big givers, are frequently

---

[1] New Revised Standard Version Bible used here and in remainder of text.

motivated by the generosity of others.

4.   The magic of ideas: the need for money is a far less effective appeal than the opportunity to launch a "new idea."

Granted the effectiveness of one or more of the above motivators, Fr. Reinert's long experience has convinced him that the most powerful motivator, one which becomes effective only over a period of time, is the spiritual benefits resulting from generous philanthropy. Giving gradually transforms a generous giver from egotistical self-centeredness to a new life, a life more closely identified both with the needy of this world and the Giver of all Good Gifts.

Spiritual Qualities in the Recipient, the Beneficiary

There can and should be a deep spiritual significance and value for the recipient of our fund-raising efforts if, as we should, we do not think of the recipient as an institution, agency, or something impersonal. That is where we make a major mistake. True, there is no spiritual essence in the strict sense in an institution itself, e.g., in buildings, libraries, retirement homes, hospital beds, or operating rooms. But these are not actually the ultimate recipient or beneficiary in the vast majority of our fund-raising efforts. In most campaigns, it is really persons, people, human beings, who are the ultimate objective and recipient, and the spiritual essence of philanthropy insofar as the *receiver* is concerned lies in the fact that we are doing something good, something important for *people*.

The depth and spiritual intensity of our personal commitment to the institution for which we are seeking money is measured and determined by our personal commitment to the recipients. No one could ever have given over forty years of his life to fund-raising for an educational institution like Saint Louis University unless he were genuinely committed to the hundreds of promising young men and women who come to us each year, whose lives now and in the future we can enrich with spiritual and material, with divine and human, possessions. So, an essential ingredient of the spiritual essence of fund-raising is the good to be accomplished by the fund-raiser's work and the donor's gift for other human beings.

The money you raise will, in God's providence, brings about a myriad of wonderfully important results: poor people here as in underdeveloped countries will gain at least a little more human dignity; handicapped children will be given some hope for a productive life; teachers will be given the opportunity to instruct young men and women how to grow spiritually, morally, intellectually, and physically; your fellow religious will be able to finish out their dedicated lives in dignity and security. In these and many other ways, by making the dollars available, the fund-raiser and the donor provide the conditions for the ministry of healing and teaching to reach those who call out for it so desperately. And this essential though indirect participation on our part should provide more than ample personal motivation, the realization of what we are accomplishing for the beneficiaries of our efforts.

CONCLUSION

Perhaps the greatest challenge to college and university presidents of the next century will be maintaining the balance of the activities and commitments briefly outlined here. The demands on administrators to engage in fund-raising will not decrease, in fact it is fair to say that whether an institution is successful or not in raising funds, there will be ever-increasing pressures on the chief administrator to locate and develop sources of support for his or her institution. Failure to meet goals will logically call for redoubled efforts, but success breeds ever higher expectations and even more pressure to find new sources of funding. Since this job is so demanding and crucial, the temptation will be to down-play the roles of academic leadership and fiscal management. This would be at least partially a mistake, for while it may be possible for a university to be financially managed with a fair degree of success by a presidential appointee, in matters of moral and intellectual leadership there is no substitute for the person of the president.

Yet along with the tremendous responsibilities which we have only briefly alluded to here come special rewards which may be difficult for any one to imagine who has not led an educational institution through good times and bad. While the demanding and sometimes competing tasks of a university president can lead to conflict, frustration, and heartache,[2] they can also be the source of great satisfaction, which can perhaps best be compared with a feeling of pride and identification with one's family. The position of university president, despite claims to the contrary, is not yet the same as being the CEO of a large corporation. While there are obvious similarities, i.e., both are responsible to a corporate Board of Trustees, to be successful both must exercise human relations, personnel management, and financial control skills, and both must be able to articulate a vision for the company or institution's future, one of the major differences is the functioning and responsibilities of a university Board of Trustees vis-à-vis the university president in contrast to a corporate board's relationship to the company's CEO. As a "public trust" a university has unique obligations to the outside community and to society in general. This requires a special governance structure whereby the Trustees serve as a policy-formation body at once committed to the mission and goals of the university, yet "detached" representatives of the society which the university is committed to serve. The president stands between the Trustees and all those who comprise "the university"—faculty, staff, and students—as both their leader and servant.

After years of service in this extremely difficult role of university president, Fr. Reinert became convinced that the traditional governance structure at Catholic universities was seriously flawed. How a more effective system of governance was achieved during his presidency is the subject of the following chapter.

---

[2] Some of the difficulties facing contemporary university presidents are addressed in Thomas Toch, "The Terrible Toll on College Presidents," *U.S. News & World Report,* 12 December 1994, p. 82.

CHAPTER FOUR

A PIONEERING VENTURE IN CATHOLIC UNIVERSITY GOVERNANCE

WHAT YOU HAVE AS HERITAGE TAKE NOW AS TASK; FOR THUS WILL YOU MAKE IT YOUR OWN.

—GOETHE

The first ten to fifteen years of experience in university governance had convinced Fr. Reinert that a private American college or university could never reach the goals which its mission was calling for without the continuing dedicated help and resources of an organized group of citizens. From the founding of the earliest college in the U.S., such groups were legally designated in civil law as trustees—a body accountable for overseeing the financial and academic responsibilities set forth in a state charter formally establishing the institution as a specified type of academic institution.

However, the governance pattern at Saint Louis University up to

47

the 1970s was typical of all Jesuit and Catholic colleges in the United States: each institution was owned and operated by the Jesuits or some other religious congregation, and the assets of the institution were considered ecclesiastical property subject to the canon law of the Church. At the same time very little recognition was being given to the fact that by reason of its civil charter from the state of Missouri, Saint Louis University was in secular circles designated as a public trust authorized by the state to grant academic degrees and to enjoy tax exemption as a not-for-profit corporation. Clearly, therefore, the University and its assets were not legally the same as a parish church or a seminary serving the interests of the Catholic Church under canon law.

By the mid-twentieth century, it was becoming obvious that the Catholic colleges and universities governed and supported almost exclusively by the human and financial resources of a religious community such as the Society of Jesus simply could not compete either with the governmentally supported public institutions nor even with the other private and church-related colleges which were being governed and supported by "outside" boards of trustees. In most instances the membership of these Boards was made up of men and women committed to forwarding the institutional mission by generous contributions in one or more of three key areas: "work, wealth, or wisdom."

Fr. Reinert's determination to find a legitimate answer to the seemingly impossible ecclesiastical and economical obstacles to the governance problem was strengthened, ironically, by Vatican Council II's redefinition of the Catholic Church as "the people of God" rather than the hierarchy and clergy. The revolutionary document "The Church in the Modern World" called for the participation and leadership of Catholic lay men and women in every facet of the church's mission, including education.

But the final achievement of a bona fide board of trustees had to be preceded by a series of preparatory, experimental changes. First, the position and authority of the president of the university needed clarification. After a relatively few years in office, Fr. Reinert became convinced that the administrative responsibilities of both university president and rector-superior of the Jesuit community were mutually incompatible. In the Society of Jesus, the rector of a community is expected to be available, to become intimately acquainted with each member through regular conferences, and to be the liaison between his community and the provincial superior. Up until Fr. Reinert's time, every preceding president had also served as rector of the community. This explains why the average tenure of every president had been six years—canon law required that a major religious superior could serve a maximum of two three-year terms.

With the endorsement of the provincial superior, Fr. Linus Thro, the authorities in Rome were petitioned to allow an experiment: the president technically remaining rector but a superior responsible to him discharging his duties vis-à-vis the Jesuit community. Fr. William Fitzgerald was appointed superior in 1952 and after fifteen years of successful experimentation, the position of president was officially separated from an authoritative relationship to the Jesuit community, and Fr. William Stauder became the first independent rector in 1967. This pattern of administration, which was first devised at Saint Louis University, is now the common practice in all American Jesuit universities, colleges, and high schools. To solidify those new relationships at Saint Louis University, a tripartite contract was developed which outlined the essential duties and responsibilities of the three corporations involved: (1) the provincial of the Missouri province; (2) the rector of the Jesuit community at Saint Louis University, and (3) the president of the university.

In the meantime, Fr. Reinert and his confreres at Saint Louis University felt called to exercise leadership in the painstaking process of bringing Saint Louis University into the mainstream of institutional governance as practiced by all well-established American colleges and universities. But while one Catholic institution would have to take the lead, it was clear that all other Jesuit and probably all other Catholic institutions would immediately be affected. Consequently, the next step taken by the university in the governance restructuring process was to initiate and sponsor countrywide discussions on the advantages and disadvantages of vesting final authority in a board of trustees including both lay and religious members, the legal implications thereof (both civil and canonical), the changed relationships between the institution and its sponsoring diocese or religious community, and, most importantly, how to safeguard the continuity of the institution specifically as a Catholic college or university.

Particularly important was a Conference of Presidents and their representatives from most of the Jesuit colleges and universities held at

Saint Louis University May 20–21, 1967. Fr. John McGrath, canon lawyer at the Catholic University of America, gave a convincing analysis of the legitimacy of restructuring governing boards and separate incorporation of religious communities from the educational institutions which they sponsor.

Also discussed was the success which Saint Louis University had experienced since 1963 with a lay Board of Trustees chaired by Dr. Ted Hochwalt, then vice president for Research at the Monsanto Company. Although this Board was in a legal sense strictly advisory, every effort had been made to have this group of twelve individuals function as though they were in fact the legally constituted ultimate university authority.

Concurrently, discussions were in process with Fr. Linus Thro, Provincial of the Missouri Province and his consultors, and these discussions were then carried on with the new Father General of the Society, Fr. Pedro Arrupe, while Frs. Thro and Fr. Reinert were in Rome attending the Thirty-First General Congregation of the Society of Jesus. Although the issue of governance was a matter largely confined to American Jesuit institutions, it proved helpful that one of the Decrees on Education issued by the Thirty-First General Congregation endorsed "the advisability of establishing Boards of Trustees composed both of Jesuits and laymen."

In the meantime, Fr. Reinert, after painstaking consultation, had decided that the best candidate for chairman of the proposed newly constituted Board of Trustees would be Daniel L. Schlafly, a St. Louis businessman who had been making an outstanding community contribution as president of the Board of the St. Louis Public School System. Independent of Fr. Reinert, Dan Schlafly characteristically probed into every aspect of the proposal, had lengthy meetings with Fr. Provincial Thro, and even went to Rome to be assured of the complete approval and support of Fr. General Pedro Arrupe.

At long last on January 21, 1967, Saint Louis University announced that it had become the first major American institution operated by a Catholic religious order to vest legal ownership and control in a Board composed of both lay persons and clergy. The initial Board included eighteen lay men and women plus ten Jesuits, all recognized locally or nationally as leaders in their respective professions or businesses. Far from a move toward "secularization," the new Trustees were explicitly chosen because of their demonstrated commitment to the mission of the

University and to the promotion of the spiritual and religious inspiration and values of the Judeo-Christian traditions and the intellectual ideals of the Society of Jesus.

The preceding matter-of-fact narration of the successful establishment of a radically new governance structure for the university does not assume that the months, even years, preceding this event were without controversy. The "laicizing" of the Board was viewed by some, including Jesuits, as a dangerous dilution of the Catholic nature and mission of the University. Critics speculated how far the changes and liberalization would be carried. Pointing to trends in universities sponsored by Protestant denominations in the country's early history, these critics traced a pattern in which originally religious schools such as Yale or Princeton gradually but steadily drifted away from their roots to become completely secularized institutions. Fr. Reinert as well as most of the Jesuit university administrators countered with the basic argument that the 1832 charter of the University was intact, that the bylaws governing the reorganized Board specify that: the University will be publicly identified as a Catholic, Jesuit university; the University will be motivated by the moral, spiritual, and religious inspiration and values of the Judeo-Christian tradition; and that the University will be guided by the spiritual and intellectual ideals of the Society of Jesus. These By Laws set a new standard for Jesuit higher education. In 1984 when Fr. Paul FitzGerald, S.J., for many years an officer in the national office of the Jesuit Educational Association (JEA), published a scholarly history of the profound changes in the governance of Catholic colleges and universities, he began with the new structure of the Board of Trustees at Saint Louis University in 1967.[1]

Now that nearly thirty years have elapsed since the move to lay participation in governance of Catholic colleges and universities, research studies report almost universal agreement that the implementation of the policy has been of substantial benefit to all Catholic institutions. Sister Alice Gallin, O.S.U., former president of the Association of Catholic Colleges and Universities, reports the results of her study of this development in a monograph to be published by the University of Notre Dame Press. This report will constitute a chapter

---

[1] Paul A. FitzGerald, S.J., *The Governance of Jesuit Colleges in the United States 1920–1970*, Notre Dame: University of Notre Dame, 1984.

in a book Sister Gallin is writing on the major developments in Catholic higher education since 1960. Her comments are reassuring: "On the basis of the research I am doing on the history of Catholic higher education since 1960, I think that it would be accurate to say that the inclusion of lay men and women on Boards of Trustees and the full empowerment of those Boards to govern Catholic colleges and universities was undoubtedly the most significant and far-reaching development in Catholic higher education in the second half of the twentieth century."

For those who remember or who were involved in any aspect of academic life during the 1960s and early 1970s, it would not be surprising to hear that the 28 "new" Saint Louis University Trustees were immediately confronted with a wide range of very serious issues: the nationwide student "revolution" initiated by the U.S.-Vietnam involvement; the need of policies to regulate the hordes of radical speakers eager to indoctrinate young students; the pressure on faculties to unionize; the trend to liberalize or eliminate regulations relating to student life on campus, coed dorms, etc.; the racial tension due to the presence of African American as well as Hispanic and Asian students; the increased need for more space in order to provide modern classroom and laboratory and housing facilities; and, most challenging of all, the frightening need for successful fund-raising campaigns to provide these needs without bankrupting the University.

Within the five-year period from 1967 to 1972, the Trustees faced each of these demands and gave evidence that the move to lay participation had been introduced none too soon. And so in 1972 Fr. Reinert informed the Board of Trustees that he thought it was wise that he step down as president as soon as the Trustees could identify a suitable replacement. While Fr. Reinert was in good health and had the energy of a man twenty years his junior, the announcement did not come entirely as a surprise to members of the Board. After over two decades of Fr. Reinert's leadership, the university was ready, as he put it, "for a change." Moreover, he was convinced he could be of greater service in terms of the university's current needs if he were freed of the time-consuming internal administrative demands in order to concentrate on two specific goals: (1) fund-raising, particularly in the area of major gifts from individuals, and (2) an effort to bring together all of the major constituents of the Midtown area—businesses, institutions sponsoring music and the fine arts, property owners, etc.—into a coalition aiming at a revitalization of the entire area enveloping both the main campus and the Medical Center of the University. Although Fr. Reinert asked that his title be that of one of the vice presidents of the University, the Trustees decided that while indeed he would be responsible to the president, his title would be that of chancellor, lest it would appear that he was being "demoted." The story of the newly constituted chancellor's "New Town" venture will be developed in Chapter VI.

Given Fr. Reinert's request in 1972 to be relieved of the presidential duties, the Board began the search for a new president. This was not easy, as Chairman Schlafly recalls, for several reasons, not the least of which was the reputation of the outgoing president and the reluctance of many possible candidates to be compared with him. Undaunted, the Board drew up a list of qualifications it wanted in a new president: experience in administration and community relations, strong academic credentials, and, most importantly, the ability to work well with a Board of Trustees. Led by Chairman Dan Schlafly, the Board conducted a nationwide search, limiting itself to Jesuit candidates in accordance with the by-laws of the newly constituted Jesuit/lay Board. The process of selection was long and arduous, but finally a local candidate was chosen: Fr. Daniel O'Connell, a professor of psychology, well-liked by students and faculty.

Fr. O'Connell entered the presidency with a great deal of goodwill and support from the University family as well as a firm commitment from Fr. Reinert to divorce himself completely from any aspect of internal University administration but to be available for advice and guidance if desired. In retrospect, Fr. Reinert is convinced it would have been wiser for him to have taken a year's sabbatical away from the University, because in spite of every effort to make it clear that he was not "the power behind the throne," many people inside or outside the University who were looking for advice, favors, or just information would bypass the president and seek out Fr. Reinert. Fr. O'Connell's position was further weakened by his lack of administrative experience. The new president made decisions that alienated faculty and administrators, and at times seemed to be unable to come to grips with the financial problems of higher education in the mid-1970s. After four years of extremely difficult administrative struggle, in 1978 Fr. O'Connell was persuaded to offer his resignation to the Board.

Another search was initiated, but in a climate of somewhat more urgency than before. Four years of less than effective leadership and sometimes public blunders had not furthered the University's prestige or improved its financial position. The Board selected Fr. Edward J. Drummond, S.J., who had had considerable experience as an administrator at Marquette and more recently in the University's Medical Center and had a reputation for sound judgment. Due to his age, Fr. Drummond understood that his tenure as president would be relatively short, but he wisely asked for and got full powers as president rather than as acting president. In the meantime, the Board created a smaller and more streamlined search committee, starting the process once again. After four years as chancellor, Fr. Reinert's identity as ex-president of the University and a non-administrator was more clearly established, making it considerably easier to conduct a search for a president who was to be his own man.

Fr. Thomas R. Fitzgerald, S.J. was chosen to lead the University and began his tenure in September 1979. At his inauguration, he outlined in some detail about five major developments which he was convinced needed to take place in the immediate future. Showing unusual persistence in pursuing his goals, and remarkable fiscal management skills, Fr. Fitzgerald in the space of eight years achieved his goals for the University and announced to the Trustees his desire to be replaced so that he could return to his first love, teaching.

In 1987 the Trustees concluded a nationwide search with the appointment of Fr. Lawrence Biondi, at that time Dean of the College of Arts and Sciences at Loyola University of Chicago and a member of Saint Louis University's Board of Trustees. His dynamic leadership during the past eight years has generated not only some substantial academic advancements in various schools of the University (including the university campus in Madrid, Spain), but an extremely impressive expansion, modernization, and beautification, particularly of the University's main Frost Campus.

Having traced in this chapter the trail-blazing developments of a unique pattern of governance for American Catholic colleges and universities, it seems important to devote the next chapter (V) to highlight the major academic developments which have taken place at Saint Louis University over the past fifty years, particularly those which would not have occurred without presidential leadership and the resources and community acceptance which the new Board of Trustees made possible.

CHAPTER
FIVE

ACADEMIC
GROWTH

THE UNIVERSITY IS DEDICATED TO LEADERSHIP IN THE
CONTINUING QUEST FOR UNDERSTANDING OF GOD'S CREATION,
AND FOR DISCOVERY, DISSEMINATION AND INTEGRATION OF THE
VALUES, KNOWLEDGE AND SKILLS REQUIRED TO TRANSFORM
SOCIETY IN THE SPIRIT OF THE GOSPELS.

—MISSION STATEMENT OF SAINT LOUIS UNIVERSITY

Schools have the potential to redefine themselves in a number of ways, including in terms of their academic and intellectual commitment. Some institutions grow broader in their defined mission; others become more specialized. The expectations which an institution holds for its members can also change. University administrators often like to talk about the "raising of academic standards" for both faculty and students, but in reality the realignment of priorities is not as simple as, for example, merely turning away a

55

higher percentage of applicants. Paralleling the physical transformation and the numerical growth of Saint Louis University has been a significant change in the way the University views and presents itself as an intellectual and academic institution. If we do not call this change a transformation, it is because the academic and intellectual growth of the University is, we believe, no revolution but a natural outcome of centuries-old Jesuit pedagogical and scholarly traditions.

As we have noted earlier, in the 1940s the University was heir to several traditions. In addition to the heritage of scholarship which had distinguished Jesuit higher education for much of the previous four centuries, there was also the more localized tradition of looking to the immediate needs of the Saint Louis Catholic community. These two traditions were by no means incompatible, but the latter had come to predominate in the minds of many University administrators and local residents. No one was actually unhappy with this arrangement, but it seems likely that in the rapidly changing post-World War II era profound change was inevitable. Looking back, it is not possible to claim that all the changes that came to the University in the postwar years were premeditated or even foreseeable, but from a distance they do seem to reflect interrelated developments in the wider world. For example, the war brought, through advances in aerial bombardment, the horrifying destruction of many irreplaceable libraries, which became one of the chief impetuses for the creation of the Vatican Microfilm Collection. Ironically, the acceleration of photographic technologies spurred on by the urgencies of war made the recreation of this resource at a site thousands of miles away possible. The arrival of former Austrian Chancellor Kurt Schuschnigg was triggered by events in Europe, and our increased awareness of these events made the contribution which Professor Schuschnigg could offer the University and the community all the more valuable and appreciated. Likewise the addition of Parks Air College to the University community was tied to the importance of airplanes in the national defense, both before and after the war. Finally, the raising of academic standards in general, and in particular the maintenance of high academic standards for collegiate athletes was dictated in part by the changes in the job market created by the postwar economy. Returning veterans had higher skill levels, higher expectations, and different needs, changing forever the acceptability of the "gentleman's C" and other holdovers from an earlier, more restricted view of higher education.

The changes related in this chapter also were consequences of more conscious efforts to move the University to a new level of what might be called institutional maturity. By roughly 1940, Saint Louis University had reached a level of service to the community and involvement in the concerns of the wider world which could not be expanded without a re-evaluation of its resources, its potential community members and its long-range goals. Once the process of expanding each of these was underway, other, previously unforeseen opportunities, stemming from combinations of new factors, presented themselves. The inclusion of veterans into the student body, for example, complemented the integration of Parks College into the University's structure. The presence of each of these new developments also propelled the University further along the course to becoming a university with national standing beyond the world of Jesuit or even Catholic institutions, a process which is continuing today. But this process required some sense of what was to happen next, and the actual story of the University during these years reflects the counterpoint between the planned outcomes of Fr. Reinert and others, and the unanticipated developments which sometimes proved to be catalysts for future growth.

VATICAN FILM LIBRARY

One of the greatest libraries in the world is housed in the Vatican City, where popes over the past five centuries, beginning with Nicholas V, have collected a stunning array of manuscripts, rare books, and other documents. An unusual set of circumstances brought an important part of the collection to St. Louis in the 1950s. Prior to World War II, Saint Louis University, despite its inclusion of a number of significant scholars on its teaching faculty, did not possess an extensive research library. The teaching emphasis of the University, the hardships of the Depression and the Second World War, and the financial constraints imposed by the limited amount of alumni support prevented the expansion of Saint Louis University's library system for many years. Yet developments in far-off Europe changed all that. During most of the Second World War, Rome and the Vatican City were spared the destruction which was inflicted on virtually every other European city. As Allied troops approached in 1944, Rome was declared an open city, which prevented the sort of last minute holocaust which leveled

Dresden and other irreplaceable cultural centers. Nevertheless, the destruction of the nearby monastery of Monte Cassino and the totality of the devastation visited upon the libraries, museums, and archives of Europe made it clear that the Vatican Library, with its priceless collection of manuscripts, incunabula, and rare documents, could have easily shared the fate of other cultural monuments that had been lost forever. Moreover, no duplicates existed for the overwhelming majority of the objects housed in the Vatican collections; if they were destroyed there would be no way even of determining what had been lost. This situation was complicated by the fact that the Vatican librarians had never compiled a complete index of their holdings, a difficulty which had long frustrated scholars using the library.

Fr. Lowrie Daly, an archivist and historian, came to President Reinert a few years after the war and suggested that the time was ripe to go to Rome and explain to Pope Pius XII the danger the Vatican Library faced if war ever again came to Italy. As a result of Fr. Daly's persuasive skills, the Pope agreed to the photographing of all the documents in the library and their transferal to microfilm. Yet even after receiving permission from the Vatican to commence reproducing documents from the Vatican Library, serious practical problems remained on both sides of the Atlantic. Fr. Reinert was still faced with the problem of financing this expensive and drawn-out process. Recognizing that the University did not possess the resources to do more than initiate such an undertaking, he turned to a University graduate and local attorney, Luke Hart, for help. Hart was Supreme Grand Knight of the Knights of Columbus, a Catholic fraternal organization with a long history of charitable activities, but few ties to the world of scholarship. Hart also had to face the skepticism of some Knights, who saw the Order's responsibility more in the area of providing insurance, but he eventually succeeded in obtaining the money needed to carry on the microfilming.

The realization that American scholars would no longer need to travel to Rome to conduct their research did not make Fr. Daly's work in Rome any easier. The Vatican librarian, concerned about the conditions under which the filming was to take place and more than willing to place obstacles in the way of the Americans, insisted that the filming process be conducted with special cameras which produced finished copies of the documents almost immediately. In the late 1940s the cameras that could perform such a task were hard to find; in the United States the only ones were in California, where they were being used by the Air Force. Father Reinert tried repeatedly to procure one of these machines but was thwarted at every turn. Only a special order from the Commander-in-Chief of the Armed Forces would make one of these expensive machines available. Hoping against hope, Fr. Reinert phoned the White House and talked with President Harry Truman, who had visited the University campus previously while his great-nephew had been a graduate student there. When Fr. Reinert reminded the President that he had complained that Easterners did not believe that there was any important body of knowledge west of the Appalachians, Truman, a native Missourian, agreed that the establishment of a Vatican collection in St. Louis would be a sizable addition to Midwestern and Missouri culture. Nor did the regulation that use of the cameras be limited to defense purposes trouble the President. He simply announced that preservation of copies of the documents in the Vatican was an act of defending a priceless part of world culture. The order was signed, and one of the filming machines was soon on its way to Rome.

Although sometimes incorrectly referred to as the "Vatican Archives," the collection obtained from Rome by the University is in fact from the holdings of the Vatican Library, the personal library of the popes. The collection housed at Saint Louis University today comprises two types of holdings: manuscripts and printed books whose total numbers more than fourteen million pages. The University also possesses over 4,000 slides of illuminated manuscripts housed in the Vatican as well as a partially complete cataloguing system begun in 1928 and carried on until the outbreak of the Second World War. Taken together, these total about 700,000 documents. In addition to the documents from the Vatican Library which were microfilmed, the University also took advantage of the opportunity to microfilm materials from the central archives of the Society of Jesus in Rome. These included documents from North and South America, and from the Philippines, and total more than a million pages. As is the case with the Vatican collection, the microfilms which the University obtained represent the only collection of its kind in the Western hemisphere.

The microfilm collection was eventually housed in the new University library, which was completed in 1958 and named in honor of Pius XII, who had died that year. Since this task was completed the Vatican Film Library has been the recipient of financial assistance from other outside sources, including the Andrew W. Mellon Foundation. The microfilm collection continues to attract researchers from many parts of the world.

PARKS COLLEGE

Of all of the "extramural" friends of the University to appear in the postwar years, aviator and entrepreneur Oliver Lafayette Parks was one of the most unusual. Not only was his background not Catholic, but his own education and interests did not suggest that he would become closely involved with a liberal arts institution. Parks first came in contact with the Jesuits in a dramatic fashion: his airplane crashed on the grounds of the Jesuit seminary at Florissant. Although Parks was not seriously hurt, his period of convalescence gave him an opportunity to get to know the Jesuits, and started a friendship with them that would eventually result in his conversion to Catholicism.

The Parks Air College was founded by Parks in 1927. The school had trained hundreds of fliers who served in the Army Air Corps in World War II, and by 1946 the campus included 22 buildings on 113 acres and was worth approximately $3 million with an enrollment of 368 students.[1] Parks himself was not college-educated, but he came to admire the Jesuit educational philosophy and the thoroughness of their training. It still came as a shock when in early 1946 Oliver Parks approached President Holloran with the idea that he give the entire college to Saint Louis University. Arguments that a technical school of this type was outside the usual mission of Jesuit higher education did not dissuade Parks; in fact, he not only insisted that the school be fully integrated into the University, but that all Parks students complete the same liberal arts requirements that other University students did. On August 23 of that year, President Holloran announced with a flourish "the affiliation of Parks Air College with the University."

Hard work lay ahead, however. Most Parks students were caught somewhat off guard by the change in administration. The faculty, many of whom were veteran pilots but who did not possess advanced degrees, had to be integrated into the traditionally academic and at this point still quite isolated University academic community. Most difficult was the integration of the course requirements of the University into the curriculum of the Parks students. In the immediate postwar years, Parks

---

[1] *St. Louis Post-Dispatch*, 23 August 1946, p. 3A.

students were predominantly veterans with wartime flying experience and a desire to make a career in the burgeoning airline industry. Like other veterans, the study of theology or philosophy was not their uppermost concern. More than many other veteran students, Parks students also frequently lacked the formal academic training necessary to succeed in a university. Only with difficulty were many of them persuaded of the necessity of a liberal arts education. There was also the problem of physically integrating the air college into the rest of the University, a difficulty that could never be completely solved until Parks will have been moved to the Frost Campus by 1997. By the mid-1950s, however, Parks was a flourishing and financially sound part of the University. The continued growth of commercial airline service in the postwar decades contributed significantly to the success of the school, as did the proximity of McDonnell Douglas, the aircraft manufacturing firm, in St. Louis. The 1960s also saw the first female student enrolled at Parks, following the trend of coeducation which had already been underway at the University some decades before.

Along with good times there were also the difficult ones, however. The airline industry is particularly susceptible to fluctuations and traditionally has operated on a slender profit margin, so when profits were down, layoffs followed. The boom in aerospace jobs promoted by changes in the travel habit of Americans and by the Vietnam War turned into an industry-wide slump in the 1980s. By the mid-1990s, despite many decades of success, serious questions about Parks' future had arisen. Enrollment had declined from over 1,000 to 600, and millions of dollars were required for the upgrading of computers and library renovations. The depression in the aerospace industry and the decline in demand for narrowly trained engineers, which few had foreseen in the previous decade, appeared to be a long-term phenomenon. While the University did not want to abandon Parks, the Board of Trustees felt that it had to take decisive action to get Parks back on what it believed was the "right track." This recommendation resulted from the growing demand for improving the infrastructure at Parks—both academic and physical—and the advantage of bringing Parks into the University community of colleges and schools.

During the early part of the academic year 1995–96, a Parks Leadership Council, consisting of the vice presidents and deans most directly involved with Parks College, developed a comprehensive plan for a "new" Parks. At the present time, this plan calls for the creation of two divisions within the school, one for aviation and aerospace sciences, one for engineering. The programs in aerospace and aviation will look similar to those we now have except that we will be moving more heavily into computer-based instruction and additional computer science requirements. The engineering division will develop the aerospace engineering option, electrical option, and the recently added mechanical option. The first is a joint program in engineering and business. This will probably be a certificate option at the undergraduate level, and a BS/MBA in engineering and business at the graduate level. The second interdisciplinary program will be in biomedical engineering. This will involve a collaboration with the Biology Department and the School of Allied Health Professions which will provide medical instrumentation courses.

As mentioned before, the restructuring of the Parks curriculum is based on the assumption that Parks physically will be relocated to the Frost Campus of the University. As of January 1998, the "new" Parks will be located on the south side of Lindell Boulevard, east of Grand. A city block between Theresa and Compton Avenues has been purchased and the buildings in that block are currently being demolished.

Cannon, Inc., the architectural firm commissioned for the task, has designed a very modern building with interior skyways which bring in natural light. The building has modern labs, "smart" classrooms, and comfortable offices to accommodate an educational program that is becoming increasingly computer-driven. The faculty have been intimately involved in its design and are excited about the prospects of a new facility.

The Department of Physics will move from Arts and Sciences into the new Parks building. Parks' Chemistry Department will move to Monsanto Hall with the Arts and Sciences' chemists. Increasingly, the applied science and mathematics people at Parks will be involved with delivering a science and mathematics curriculum that is geared specifically for the "new" engineer and aviator. That means they will be expected to work in interdisciplinary teams in a problem-focused curriculum. One might say that we are applying the Harvard Business School model of curriculum innovation to aviation and engineering. Aviation flight and mechanical training programs will remain at Cahokia, in an expanded airport hangar facility.

The "vision" for Parks is this: the modern university, especially the Catholic university, must be immersed in the problems of science and technology. The problems which plague mankind today are to some extent created by modern technology, just as they are ameliorated and solved by technology. Since the 150th anniversary of the founding of the University, Saint Louis University has been grappling quite explicitly with the issue of "man" (and woman) and technology. Parks has been known for its pioneering position in one of the technological worlds—aviation—and the "new" Saint Louis University intends to build on that foundation. One should probably say that the present health and vigor of the University allows us to move forward into engineering and technology with some of the same conviction and hope that we have in the other sciences, especially the health sciences and the social services.

With Parks on "this side of the river," students and faculty will be able to take advantage of the strong program in the humanities, the social sciences, and health-related disciplines. Programs are being designed to expand the computer science program. Parks will be the home of a computer science department giving foundational courses to students in business, allied health, nursing, and mathematics. Faculty in medicine and at Parks are designing a biomedical engineering program. Undergraduate students will be able to work in the sophisticated labs of the medical center and hospitals throughout the region as interns and as participants in research projects attempting to refine and improve our health apparatus and information systems. Students from both Parks and from Business and Administration will have the opportunity to double-major in business and engineering. Faculty from both schools have already decided that the strong humanities core will remain a special feature of these Saint Louis University graduate programs.

The new Parks will anchor the eastern end of the campus. Because of the numbers of students and faculty who will be making the new building their home, a parking facility for 1,500 cars will be constructed in what is now Laclede Town. This will clear the central campus, east of Grand Boulevard, of all traffic. Fr. Biondi's vision is to create several malls on the east side of the campus, the first running alongside the new Parks and starting at the corner of Grand and Lindell, to imitate the beautiful "western" half of Frost Campus. With the science buildings close by, the eastern side of Grand will be known as the "science and technology" end of campus.

The new facility, the parking structure, and new malls will be a major investment in the revitalization of Midtown and the old Mill

Creek area, and will complete the campus. The many millions of dollars that are being invested here speak of the University's commitment to the city and to its belief that the University can be one of the most significant and most positive forces for growth and revitalization because it has exactly the right thing to offer to this formerly blighted area: education and training in a humanistic tradition, or more simply, "hope."

DR. KURT SCHUSCHNIGG

The upheavals of the Second World War drove many prominent European intellectuals and political leaders to the safety of the United States, where many of them, from Albert Einstein to Béla Bartók, continued to have productive careers. Most who found positions in academia settled on the East Coast, although a few traveled further into the heartland of the country. The most notable of these displaced Europeans who reached Saint Louis University in the 1940s was Dr. Kurt Schuschnigg, who was also the only former head of state ever to teach at the University. Schuschnigg's career was in many ways paradoxical and even controversial, reflecting the times in which he lived. He was born in 1897, the son of a general in the old Austro-Hungarian army and heir of an ennobled family. Educated by Jesuits in Feldkirch and elsewhere in Austria, Schuschnigg served in the Austro-Hungarian army during the First World War and was decorated several times. Following the Austro-Hungarian Empire's defeat and dismemberment, Schuschnigg trained as a lawyer and soon entered politics in the shrunken and politically unstable Republic of Austria. Staunchly conservative and pro-Catholic, with monarchist leanings, Schuschnigg aligned himself with the Christian-Socialist Party, led by Engelbert Dolfuss. In the early 1930s after Dolfuss became Chancellor and virtual dictator, Schuschnigg served in the Austrian cabinet as Minister of Education and as Minister of Justice.

In July of 1934 Austrian Nazi thugs acting with German backing attempted a coup and assassinated Chancellor Dolfuss. The coup quickly proved unsuccessful and a few days later Schuschnigg became the new Chancellor. While not as absolute a ruler as Dolfuss, Schuschnigg favored a rightist course, restoring property of the exiled Hapsburg dynasty and visiting Italian dictator Benito Mussolini several times. As Europe drifted toward war, Schuschnigg's attempts to steer a course between his two totalitarian neighbors proved futile. By 1938 German pressure on Austria to join the Reich had become intense, and after browbeatings from Hitler and civil disturbances in several Austrian cities, Schuschnigg reluctantly agreed to allow a plebiscite to determine if Austria should be annexed by Germany. In an election whose voting regulations made it almost impossible to vote "no," Austrians voted overwhelmingly for union with the Reich and Schuschnigg resigned, to spend the war years in Nazi detention camps. In 1947 he emigrated to the United States with his family, and shortly after his arrival he accepted a post at Fordham University as a professor of political science. However, he did not remain long in New York. Harassed by critics who branded him a collaborator of the Nazis, Schuschnigg found it impossible to continue his teaching responsibilities, and might have returned to Europe permanently if it had not been for an old friend who had started a new career in this country. Dr. William H. Bauer, an Austrian physician and old friend of Schuschnigg, came to Saint Louis University in 1938, owing to his Jewish ancestry and his anti-Nazi stance. He taught in the Schools of Medicine and Dentistry concurrently, and following Schuschnigg's arrival in the United States, urged him to come to Saint Louis University. Schuschnigg was familiar with the University from a visit the previous year, and in 1948 began a career as a professor of political science and history which lasted eighteen years.

Schuschnigg was praised by some for averting the inevitable violence that would have resulted from any attempt to resist the Nazi takeover, while others criticized his failure to defend Austrian Jews and his cool relations with the Socialists. On more than one occasion he was denounced as a fascist and a tool of the Nazis, but Fr. Reinert was always supportive of the Austrian émigré and in 1968 awarded him the fleur-de-lis, the university's highest honor. Dr. Schuschnigg defended his actions in a book entitled *Im Kampf gegen Hitler*, which was published in 1971 in English as *The Brutal Takeover*. Contemporary *University News* stories describe Schuschnigg as a courtly and reserved teacher with a strong accent, courteous and somewhat formal by Midwestern standards, a deeply religious man who preferred not to discuss his time in office and his confinement in Dachau. Dr. Schuschnigg retired from teaching and returned to Austria in 1967, but made one final visit to St. Louis, where his wife is buried, to deliver a lecture at Saint Louis University. He died in a country home in his beloved Tyrol on

November 18, 1979. Dr. Schuschnigg's papers, including many documents relating to his term as Chancellor, are housed in the University Archives.

Many other faculty were involved in scholarship, research, and writing in the era of the 1940s when the vast majority of university professors did not regularly engage in these activities. Some of the fields where Saint Louis University faculty made important contributions were traditional areas of Jesuit scholarship: history, for example, where Saint Louis University professors produced the *Historical Bulletin;* philosophy and theology, two other Jesuit strongholds, were also well staffed with scholars. Saint Louis University faculty also were active in scientific endeavors. At the Medical School, Dr. Edward A. Doisy, Sr. conducted research on the isolation of vitamin K, for which he shared the Nobel Prize for physiology and medicine in 1943. Geophysics was another area where Saint Louis University excelled. Father James B. Macelwane, S.J., introduced seismology and founded Saint Louis University's department of geophysics, the first college department in this subject in the Western hemisphere. These researchers and scholars also supported strong graduate programs in a number of areas. The Medical School, in particular, had a long history of attracting researchers who also served as teachers. Fr. Alphonse Schwitalla, S.J., who received a Ph.D. in zoology from Johns Hopkins in 1921, was dean of the School of Medicine from 1927 to 1948 and was instrumental in attracting first-rank researchers and teachers to that institution. Another leader in research and teaching at the Medical School was Dr. Daniel M. Schoemaker, who did pioneering work in anatomy.

Although Saint Louis University in the 1940s was directed by an all-male religious group, women were an important part of the University community. For a long time nuns had been coming to Saint Louis University to obtain teaching licenses. In addition many women entered the University nursing program, whose enrollment expanded after the United States entered the war. Women students were also scattered through the departments of the College of Arts and Sciences, with a much smaller number found in the Schools of Medicine, Law, and Business. Women instructors in the 1940s, though, were a rarity. A few women taught lower-division courses in the English Department and in a few other departments in the College of Arts and Sciences. In the School of Social Work, Dr. Katharine Radke achieved international renown for her work.

DISCONTINUANCE OF TWO SCHOOLS

Along with these efforts to expand its base, the University also had to face the reality that some of the directions in which it was trying to grow were not proving to be successes. Spurred by early advances in geophysics, the University established the Institute of Geophysical Technology in 1944 (Geophysical was dropped from the name in 1948). The Institute offered an undergraduate program in several branches of engineering which sought accreditation from the Engineering Council for Professional Development. But on being informed that undergraduate accreditation would not be forthcoming until the University was firmly committed to advancing quickly into graduate programs in engineering, the University reluctantly decided that the Institute of Technology engineering program would have to be discontinued because there was no assurance that the substantial resources needed for a strong graduate program would be available. In November 1968 the name of the Institute was changed to the School of Engineering and Earth Science, and this School was phased out at the end of the 1970–71 academic year. As described earlier, the "re-birth" of Parks College as it moves to the Frost Campus will also be the equivalent of a resurrection of the Institute of Technology.

The fate of the School of Dentistry was in some ways similar to that of the Institute of Technology. The origins of the Dental School stretched back to the early part of the century, and at one point the School had played an important role in the professional life of the city. In the postwar era, however, the School of Dentistry found itself in stiff competition with other programs in the state, and under fire for the drain on resources which it placed on the rest of the University. Today the successor to the DDS program is an extremely strong graduate program in orthodontics. Nationally known, plans are currently underway to add equally strong programs leading to advanced degrees in endodontics.

INTERCOLLEGIATE ATHLETICS

"With the exception of my good friend Fr. Ted Hesburgh at Notre Dame, I doubt that many former presidents of American universities would list their involvement in athletic programs as among their most satisfying and uplifting experience. I consider myself most fortunate in my quite intimate

relationship with Billiken sports, even though in my first year as president I found it necessary to bring the football program to an inglorious demise. My predecessor, Fr. Pat Holloran, had dreamed of Saint Louis University becoming another Notre Dame powerhouse by including in the avalanche of World War II G.I.s a large number of athletes who had played football in the military under the tutelage of Joe Maniaci, himself one of the famous Fordham "blocks of granite." There were many other reasons for the failure of the program, but the chief reason was that here at Saint Louis University we did not provide an academic program that was geared to the interests, capabilities, and limitations of typical college football players—no majors in physical education, coaching, restaurant supervision, etc. Moreover, with a very small, deteriorating stadium, even a winning football team would have been a financial drain on the University's finances. While at the moment I was most unpopular among the athletes and sports fans, I was amazed in later years to be complimented even by the Dinosaurs (former Saint Louis University football players) for cutting off the program precisely to preserve both the academic and the financial integrity of the University. And from that rough beginning, intercollegiate athletics, especially basketball and soccer, has been a proud and educationally sound ingredient of the Saint Louis University experience. So much so that, while achieving national prominence in both basketball and soccer, at the same time we have been able to establish a very unique Hall of Fame on campus which celebrates and perpetuates both the athletic and academic achievements of our students. In recent years, Saint Louis University has ranked among the top 10 Division I NCAA universities in the number of our athletes who have completed all of their academic requirements and graduated from the University. I know from widespread personal contacts that the integrity of our athletic programs, fitting without apology into our Jesuit philosophy of education, has exercised a powerfully positive influence, first and foremost, on our athletes, but also on the rest of the student body and alumni, friends, and benefactors."

Nowhere is the experience of African American college students debated more intensely than in the area of collegiate sports. Critics of collegiate sports, including Berkeley sociologist Harry Edwards, have long argued that African Americans are exploited by universities that make use of their talents and then allow them to drop out or graduate without the requisite skills to pursue a career after sports. For every African American (or white) college athlete who goes to the pros, there are dozens who emerge from the experience with little to show for their efforts.[2] Although Saint Louis University long ago eliminated varsity football, the possibility has remained that the recruiting of basketball players from disadvantaged backgrounds could create dilemmas for a university committed to academics. The University has, however, continued its firm position that all athletes meet and maintain academic standards, a position which has certainly disappointed some fans from time to time and which no doubt cost the University alumni donations, but which has ultimately benefited the players and the University itself. The question continues as to how much assistance any student, black or white, who arrives at the University with areas of academic weaknesses, should receive, and where the responsibility for promoting student success lies. Coaches, professors, and tutors at the University are all called upon to assist students who may be at risk, but the issue will not go away as long as the quality of American secondary schools is so inconsistent, and as long as high school athletes are not given adequate academic guidance and encouragement.

The significance of each of the above examples of academic growth goes beyond the historical. Today Saint Louis University is reaping the results of the preliminary steps toward institutional maturity which we had just described. In March of 1994 the University was designated a Research II institution by the Carnegie Foundation for the Advancement of Teaching. This designation means that the level of research and the scale of doctoral programs at the University place it in a category with a small number of other universities which are ranked directly behind the handful of elite research institutions in the nation. Among U.S. Catholic universities, only Georgetown and Notre Dame share in this designation. This achievement is both an honor and a responsibility. The honor stems from the recognition that Saint Louis University is conducting research on a par with some of the outstanding universities in this country. The responsibility comes both from the increased visibility which follows from the Research II label and from the added responsibility of honoring the earlier commitments to teaching while living up to the new commitments of research. The roots planted in the postwar years continue to address both categories, expanding educational opportunities while in all areas strengthening the more strictly research potential of the University. We salute the

---

[2] Harry Edwards, *Black Students* (New York: The Free Press, 1970), pp. 146–147.

accomplishment of the University and wish the University continued success in both these endeavors.

CHAPTER

SIX

UNIVERSITY

AS SERVANT

AND THE LORD SAID UNTO CAIN, WHERE IS ABEL THY BROTHER? AND HE SAID, I KNOW NOT. AM I MY BROTHER'S KEEPER?

—GENESIS 4:9

WE ARE WORKERS, NOT MASTER BUILDERS, MINISTERS, NOT MESSIAHS. WE ARE PROPHETS OF A FUTURE NOT OUR OWN.

—OSCAR ROMERO

Before exploring Fr. Reinert's personal philosophy regarding the service or servant role of Saint Louis University specifically, it might be helpful to begin with a brief historical background. The earliest universities did not have what we would call campuses. Medieval scholars met in houses of professors, in rented dwellings, in disused abbeys and monasteries, or wherever they could. The university, rather than being a geographical location, was a community of individuals committed to common goals. To a significant degree, European universities have continued this tradition. There are districts in Paris, London, or Vienna where the buildings of the university cluster, but clear boundaries do not always mark the beginning of the university proper and the end of the outside world. By contrast, American colleges and universities have more often than not chosen to define their physical boundaries, to create a different environment within those boundaries, and to see themselves as geographical communities. Even in our largest cities, where space is at a premium, universities strive to create some sort of physical definition of their communities.

The creation of a campus, of a space recognizable as the university, has both potential pluses and minuses. For those who work and live within the precincts of a clearly defined urban university campus, there is a sense of community, of safety, and frequently of heightened emphasis on aesthetics in contrast to the surrounding city. Green spaces, fountains, and works of art add to the ambiance and support the notion that the university stands for something more uplifting and idealistic than the characteristically American urban values of pursuit of wealth, speed, and convenience. At the same time the difference between the campus and the surrounding neighborhood can send a message to the neighbors of the university that this is not a place for them. More important, however, than the physical difference between the campus and the surrounding community are the other messages that the university sends. It cannot be denied that many of this country's most distinguished universities are located in unsafe, impoverished, and alienated sections of our cities, whose residents have little hope of entering the university community except in the most menial capacity. Institutions that a century or two ago considered themselves to be at least partially integrated into their surrounding communities are now profoundly divorced from the concerns of these communities. Nor is this problem simply one of conflicting goals. The American campus ideal, practiced for decades by students and enshrined in movies, books, and television, is an open, trusting community, where strangers talk to one another, doors are often left unlocked, and the safety precautions dictated by modern urban life are overlooked. When this tradition collides with the "mean streets" ethos of today's cities, tragedy may result, and shock and fear turns to mistrust and hatred. The dilemma of the contemporary urban university is how to respond to the legitimate threat of harm to its members while fulfilling its mission of service to its neighbors.

Of course, not all universities have viewed the problem in this fashion. As urban neighborhoods became more unsafe, or perhaps only changed in ethnic or socio-economic composition, some of the greatest universities became fortresses, isolated and self-contained. This response is understandable, given the very real dangers that face members of the university, but we assert that there are other valid responses to the alienation of university and neighborhood which do not jeopardize the research and teaching functions of the university. Let us first, however, be candid, and admit that as expensive and difficult as it is to turn an urban campus into a defensive citadel, even more effort is required to keep it open and to keep service a high priority. Racism and prejudice, on both sides, are impediments to cooperation between town and gown. The very successes which an ambitious university experiences in the competitive world of academics pull the university away from its surrounding community, not simply in physical terms, but in the minds of teachers and students who receive no external encouragement to engage in service to others. Service, like teaching, often resists easy quantification, and it is not possible to produce a list of the top ten service universities. Moreover, the selection process of graduate school does little or nothing to develop a sense of social responsibility in the newly minted Ph.D. On the contrary, the isolation and specialization of the dissertation experience and the fierce competition to find and keep a teaching position breeds a pragmatic careerism that leaves little room for service. Even in those disciplines which concern themselves with problems of modern urban life, there is the constant risk of coming to objectify the neighbors of the university, to regard their life circumstances as problems to solve rather than human conditions to be understood. The difference in culture between the parties of the encounter can result in misunderstandings. On the side of the community, efforts by university members to assist in community projects may be interpreted as patronizing, uninformed, and self-serving. Hostility toward the institution which sponsors the service can be so great as to block any acceptance of it.

Yet service can and must be an integral part of the mission of the university, even as the university expands its physical boundaries into the community. This point is especially important as Saint Louis University continues to expand its physical boundaries and to grow in size and wealth, and in its connections with a world that lies far beyond its immediate neighborhood. The distractions of success and the lures of the materialistic culture around us combine with the pressures of living and working within a large human organization to push service into the background or to make it seem a mere ancillary to academic learning. But service to others provides the best possible avenue for the greatest goals of a university education: the challenging of accepted paradigms, the strengthening and deepening of beliefs previously held only in the abstract, and the development of personal values. Patrick Byrne, who is the founder of the PULSE service learning program at Boston College, writes of the challenges, even crises presented to students holding paradigms of justice and love when these students become engaged in service.[1] The outcomes of such encounters are far from predictable or quantifiable, and the results may not be apparent, even to the student, for a long time. Nevertheless, these outcomes can be life-changing. When coupled with the study of philosophical or theological texts which examine ethics and human motivations, the experience of service bring to life the complexities and the unifying themes of the integration of the *vita contempletiva* and the *vita activa*.

Service to the community must be complemented by an on-campus climate that recognizes and validates the community even when faculty and students are not directly engaged in work in that community. Here urban universities walk a fine line, for as they work to make their campuses safer, more beautiful and more clearly defined, they can easily shut their neighbors out.

While fully aware of the physical and psychological problems which an "open" urban university campus must grapple with today, Fr. Reinert is still committed to the "University as Servant" philosophy. In February of 1982 at the annual convention of the Association of Catholic Colleges and Universities, he endeavored to describe the basis for his University-Servant philosophy and gave illustrative examples of faculty and student initiatives both during his twenty-five years as president and his sixteen years as chancellor:

While this may represent the heretical viewpoint of an educator who has been around far too long, I have come to the conviction that the president of

---

[1] Patrick H. Byrne, "Paradigms of Justice and Love," *Conversations* 7 (Spring 1995).

any college or university today can best describe the mission of his or her institution in Biblical terms: my college, my university comes to serve, not to be served.

Years ago in the early days of my university administration, I would have been much more hesitant to cast an academic institution in the role of a servant. I was very conscious then of the faculty's sincere and legitimate concern that a college or university must always protect its primary goals of teaching and research, that over-emphasis on service can erode academic quality. I used to be worried, too, that students and non-academic personnel might become so involved in social and community-oriented programs that the primacy of learning would be threatened. While these are still legitimate concerns of mine, I have come to a conviction that in a very true sense, service is not just a third distinct subordinate function of an academic community, but in many instances service is so integral and essential to the teaching-learning process itself that the quality of these principal purposes of a college or university can actually suffer unless administrators, faculty and students generally engage in some carefully planned, targeted, and controlled forms of community service.

In other words, service programs that are integrated with the fundamental goals of a college or university need not lead to control or undue influence from outside individuals or institutions, nor result in some outside force imposing its own economic, political, or moral persuasions on the institution. Actually, such carefully monitored service programs can enhance and strengthen immeasurably the quality of teaching and research within the institution. Being at the service of the community need not result in vitiating the teaching-learning process, much less in becoming a slave of the community.

Furthermore, I would argue that if service is the generic mission of any college or university with teaching, learning, and research the specific functions within that generic mission, it should follow, it seems to me, that the service mission ought to be transcendentally appropriate for a Catholic college or university. In fact, the most distinctive quality of a Catholic college or university might well be precisely the fact that it takes its mission of Christian service to all members of its community far more seriously than its secular counterparts.

In recent years, some Jesuit colleges and universities have capsulized their educational mission as one of developing and educating "Men and Women for Others."

STUDENTS AT THE SERVICE OF THE COMMUNITY

In the aforementioned address before the Association of Catholic Colleges and Universities, Fr. Reinert developed in some detail how the "Servant" philosophy of education was being increasingly embraced by both residential and commuter students as well as by the faculty and staff.

Years ago when I was teaching a course on modern educational philosophies, I would rant and rave against John Dewey, whose theory of "learning by doing" was in our view overly pragmatic, anti-intellectual, too worldly. It's still all of that, but there was a large grain of truth in Dewey's thought that I think much of our education, especially in the liberal arts and sciences, has neglected. In a nutshell, humans learn better if **theory** *and* **practice** *can be assimilated more or less simultaneously. It is for this reason that I suggest that the learning experiences of a typical college student can be revolutionized if a serious, consistent effort is made to provide an* **environment** *in which theory and practice confront him or her at every turn.*

Suppose, for example, that the staff of the campus ministry office and of the office of student life or student development exercised every ingenuity in getting across to students that what they are learning in class, be it in religious studies, education, history, sociology, chemistry, or biology—that new knowledge can and should be applied here and now to strengthen the fabric of the college community, to make the residential halls more truly a home-away-from-home, to test the theories their professors are expounding as to what really contributes to the quality of human life and what tends to destroy it. This kind of programmed service approach can lead, for example, to students deciding themselves to improve and decorate their rooms and public spaces in the residence halls, to greater respect for property, more sincere consideration for the needs and concerns of others, legitimate pride in student accomplishments which are of service to others. Fraternities, sororities, and other student organizations can reach a point where service to others becomes the hallmark of distinction.

But in all of these applications, I think it is very important to keep students aware not just of their own campus enclave but of the greater community off-campus with which they should strive to be identified in the role of servant. The examples of this kind I have seen develop on our campus are numerous. If every day large groups of students leave the campus after classes, gather up grade school kiddies just home from school, transport them to a neighborhood center, tutor those who are falling behind because of little or no help in their own one-parent or working parents' home, give other groups of very talented boys and girls the added incentive they need to overcome boredom and to develop a vision of what might be possible for them—when college students who are regularly serving in this type of tutorial and counseling environment come back the next day to their classes in scripture, social studies, economics, communications—I can tell you their desire to learn, to question, to search has to be more acute and realistic than without this service experience. This is not just a conviction growing out of my own personal observations—it reflects the living testimony of many a graduating senior who has told me: "I learned more through my tutorial experience than any other thing that happened to me here. My experience with these kids changed my whole attitude toward my own life."

Admittedly, it takes a lot of imagination and work to provide and motivate most of the students in a college to become involved in one kind or other of service programs, but the demographics of today's society seem to guarantee we will all have unlimited service outlets: thousands of children growing up in inadequate home environment; thousands of elderly who are confined, lonely and dependent; thousands of communities with substandard living conditions; thousands of the poor who cannot afford needed legal and medical services; many who need and want to revive a religious belief that formerly supported them; hundreds of boys and girls, deserted or abused by parents, who need someone to share with, to show them personal Christian love and concern.

THE FACULTY AT THE SERVICE OF THE COMMUNITY

I suppose that the normal faculty reaction to the notion of being at the service of the community would be: so what's new? What else are we doing but serving the academic community by sharing our knowledge and wisdom with others? Granted the teachers and researchers in our institutions are performing an invaluable service just in preserving, enhancing, and communicating our intellectual tradition; nevertheless, there may be a lesson our faculties should have learned and now overlook, especially from the student movements of the sixties. Clearly, teaching today must be more than information-giving; it must be self-giving. A great teacher shares not only what he knows, but what he is. A college student today typically may be just as interested in learning what makes his chemistry teacher "tick" as in chemistry itself. After asking through the years hundreds of men and women who have been out of college for a long time: "for what are you most grateful to your alma mater," always the response centers on one or two teachers who had a great influence on their personal values, one or two men or women, who, as one grad put it, "was the first person I ever met who was almost a perfect combination of Christian faith, worldly wisdom, and compassionate love."

Self-giving by faculty, therefore, is their service par excellence, but today faculty service must also look beyond the individual student and the classroom. There are so many ways in which a teacher can give his or her students immediate responsibilities for testing their knowledge or theories in the cauldron of life experience. Internships, as required elements of an academic program, need not be confined to the more obvious majors such as business, journalism, engineering, social work, and nursing. With a little imagination experiential learning programs can be provided for students interested in oral and written communications, history and literature, even in philosophy and theology! The service aspect of such experiences always has a two-fold result: the student learns better and more, and a service is provided to individuals or institutions that otherwise would not have been available.

Obviously, faculty members can serve the broader community not only indirectly through their students, but directly by placing their knowledge, expertise, and skills at the service of companies, institutions or individuals. Everyone knows such service must be subordinated to the more important service a faculty member owes his students and his own professional self-improvement. But my experience argues that by and large the teacher, who does at least limited service for the broader community, tends to be a humbler, more convincing mentor than the one who is reluctant, so to speak, to get his hands dirty.

The Administration and President at the Service of the Community

Finally, the role of servant has been possibly *the* predominant characteristic of Fr. Reinert's tenure at Saint Louis University, both as president and later as chancellor. While the discharging of the burdensome internal duties of the president's office (as described in Chapter III) can only be honestly described as more of a burden than one human being should be asked to bear, Fr. Reinert nevertheless increasingly felt driven to exercise the leadership required to place the University and his own personal abilities at the service of the St. Louis metropolitan community.

Following in more or less chronological order are a few instances of his involvement in initiatives aimed at area-wide growth and development while strengthening the economic, educational, and social status of each of the cultural groups within the area.

KETC-TV—St. Louis Educational Television

One of the earliest and far-reaching examples of inter-University cooperation began in the 1950s when Arthur Holly Compton, Chancellor of Washington University, and Fr. Reinert agreed to develop a joint proposal to the FCC for a license to operate an educational television station in St. Louis. Working with a group of citizens headed by Ray Witcoff, each university offered substantial assets that made it possible for KETC-TV Channel 9 to begin its successful history as one of the earliest public television stations in the United States. Washington University loaned without charge a valuable piece of property at Millbrook Avenue and Big Bend Boulevard for erection of the station's studios and offices, and Saint Louis University offered use of its WEW radio tower, which was located immediately east of Chouteau House on what was then the future site of the Pius XII Memorial Library. Currently serving one of the largest viewing audiences of any educational television station, KETC is planning to move to Grand Center, the performing arts area immediately north of Saint Louis University's Frost Campus. It is to be fervently hoped that the current cut-back of governmental support for the Public Broadcasting System will not prevent KETC from moving into a modern structure with state-of-the-art equipment. Fortunately, the board and staff leadership of KETC are determined to break ground at the chosen site on Olive Street between Spring Avenue and Grand Boulevard. The establishment in Grand Center of a state-of-the-art KETC-TV headquarters and studio production building adjacent to the Pulitzer Art Museum would not only assure the future of Grand Center, but would provide new exciting educational and research opportunities for Saint Louis University.

Urban Consolidation

In 1956 through personal contacts at the Ford Foundation, Fr. Reinert was instrumental in securing a grant of $250,000, which was supplemented by a McDonnell Aircraft grant of $50,000, for a research study to be made by the departments of political science at Washington and Saint Louis Universities to study the problem of the fractionated government in the Greater St. Louis region: a small city area incapable of annexing a single foot of land beyond Skinker Boulevard (putting Washington University *outside* the city) and a St. Louis County strangling the diminutive city on three sides with over one-hundred incorporated villages and a large unincorporated area, each with its own mayor or manager, police and fire departments, etc. This largely unplanned growth began 90 years earlier when in 1876 a smug St. Louis City divorced itself from financial responsibility for the surrounding communities.

Out of the original Ford Foundation study came a series of consolidation proposals—District Plan, Burroughs Plan, etc., none of which could muster sufficient voter support to create a new municipal government for the entire metropolitan area. In the meantime, in spite of its many advantages as an urban area, the city of St. Louis had been steadily losing population and suffering from a deteriorating school system, crumbling infrastructure, etc. Recently, the Regional Commerce and Growth Association has initiated a major effort to attract new businesses into the metropolitan area, with the hope that commercial and industrial consolidation will necessarily lead to the imperative of greater governmental interdependence. The desperate need for governmental consolidation was eloquently pointed out as recently as January 7, 1995, by former Senator Thomas Eagleton on the occasion of his sharing the St. Louis Man of the Year Award with retiring Senator John Danforth.

The desperate need for urban consolidation was underlined recently by statistics from the U.S. Census Bureau: while the entire metropolitan area now has a population of 2.5 million (17th largest in the U.S.), St. Louis city proper continues to lose population to the point that the city has dropped to the 43rd place in the nation, a 44-year continuous population decline.

NATIONAL CONFERENCE OF CHRISTIANS AND JEWS

Fr. Reinert held the basic philosophy that an urban university, especially one driven by the social principles of a Catholic Jesuit institution, must use its resources and energy in area-wide efforts to develop a community where peace and justice are dominant goals. During the last 35 years, the evidence of this persistent effort has been varied and impressive. One organization with significant impact has been the National Conference of Christians and Jews (NCCJ). NCCJ sponsored interfaith activities in St. Louis as early as the 1930s, although a regional office was not established in St. Louis until 1945. The first ongoing interfaith program was initiated in 1958 when several religious leaders, including Fr. Reinert and Fr. Trafford Maher of Saint Louis University, established a Breakfast Dialogue group. This group has continued to meet bimonthly for 37 years, reportedly the oldest continuous dialogue group in the country. This program, as well as other NCCJ programs, began with efforts to resolve religious controversies, and then broadened the sphere of their concern to include racial and ethnic tensions. In 1963 the membership of the Dialogue Group included black community leaders such as Harold Woods of the *St. Louis Sentinel* and Dr. John Ervin, dean of the School of Education at Washington University. In 1978 women community leaders of the stature of Frankie Freeman, Henrietta Friedman, and Margaret Sonnenday were invited to join. Over the years many potentially serious disputes have been anticipated by this group and either have been greatly mitigated or even entirely dissipated.

THE INSTITUTE FOR PEACE AND JUSTICE

The Institute for Peace and Justice, currently celebrating its twenty-fifth anniversary, is an outgrowth of Jim McGinnis's involvement in the anti-war movement while he was a part-time faculty member at Saint Louis University in the 1970s. In search of something to balance the ROTC military studies program, Jim obtained a grant from Fr. Reinert to form the Institute for the Study of Peace. Several years later, Jim and his wife Kathy severed university connections to establish the Institute for Peace and Justice (IPJ), which has broadened its concern for world peace to include issues of racial justice. Father Reinert, who as a Board member continued his interest in and support of IPJ, was honored at the Institute's April 1995 twenty-fifth anniversary celebration as one of twelve "elders" who have been sources of renewed hope, inspiration, and energy in following Pope Paul VI's mandate: "If you want peace, work for justice."

LACLEDE TOWN

The Mill Creek Redevelopment project, which began in 1959, was one of the largest urban redevelopment projects ever sponsored by the federal government. The project involved the "Mill Creek Valley" area, which was bounded roughly by Union Station between 18th and 20th on the east, Lindell-Olive on the north, the railroad properties on the south, and Grand Avenue on the west. Practically all of the existing housing was bulldozed, and in 1964 a new community was built that was called Laclede Town. Described as "a small college town," "a safe village," and "an experiment in international living," Laclede Town was, during its halcyon days, a remarkable community which included students and faculty from Washington and Saint Louis Universities, black and white community leaders, lawyers and other professionals. But after a well-managed regime of ten to fifteen years during which the residents conscientiously controlled their own environment, Laclede Town disintegrated into a clutter of garbage, poor maintenance, and crime. Thirty years after Laclede Town's glorious beginning, more than two-thirds of the houses are boarded up and practically none of the housing is salvageable.

At the present time it has been decided that almost all structures in Laclede Town will be razed, while the future of the high-rise in Breakthrough East has not yet been decided. Several plans for the redevelopment of Laclede Town's 53 acres have been proposed and will continue to be studied. Two factors will carry much weight in the decision-making as to what the future of Laclede Town will be: the critical need for affordable new housing within the city limits of St. Louis and the expansion needs of its neighbors, particularly Saint Louis University, Harris-Stowe State College, and Berea Presbyterian Church.

NEWTOWN/SAINT LOUIS, INC.

Immediately after being relieved of his duties as president in 1974, Fr. Reinert as chancellor rallied the support of several local businesses and institutions to organize NewTown/Saint Louis, Inc. (NT/SL), a not-for-profit development organization. The goal of NT/SL was to revitalize the Midtown area by improving the quality of life for its residents, businesses, and institutions by assuring the safety and appearance of the area. NT/SL facilitated public/private partnerships, assisted in the preservation and renovation of existing viable buildings, and stimulated interest and reinvestment in the area. NT/SL also published a bimonthly newsletter, monitored and assisted redevelopment efforts, sponsored seminars and conferences, and provided assistance to local businesses, organizations, and institutions.

Perhaps its most important contribution since its creation in 1974 was the leadership it exerted in the formation of three separate, independent, limited-for-profit, redevelopment corporations: the Lafayette Towne Redevelopment Corporation (now known as the Gate District in Saint Louis), the Midtown Medical Center Redevelopment Corporation (which will be discussed in the following section), and the City Center Redevelopment Corporation (CCRC). Each of these redevelopment corporations is still implementing a specific redevelopment plan within the boundaries of NT/SL.

CCRC, the most recent redevelopment corporation growing out of the original NT/SL institution, was incorporated in 1980, with the original shareholders being: Saint Louis University, The Urban League of Metropolitan Saint Louis, Saint Louis Symphony Society, Third Baptist Church, Scottish Rite Masons, Mercantile Bank, and Centerre Bank (now Boatmen's Bank).

The focus and intent of this redevelopment effort was to utilize the existing buildings (theaters, high-rise doctors' office buildings, fraternal halls) and the heritage of the area to recreate the arts and entertainment district for Saint Louis. CCRC would act as an umbrella redeveloper by attracting other private development interests to take on specific projects and by coordinating the thematic development within this district. It was believed that an independent, civic-minded Board would best represent the existing property owners within the area and protect the interests of the smaller business and property owners in the district while at the same time encouraging them to reinvest and upgrade their properties.

Fr. Reinert approached both Mercantile and Centerre banks with a five-year request to assist in underwriting this effort. He leveraged Saint Louis University's commitment of $35,000 a year with a matching offer from each bank to buy $35,000 in stock annually to underwrite operations. In 1981 the Board of Aldermen adopted the plan and the 353 redevelopment rights were vested in CCRC. At this same time, Fox Associates began to explore development of the Fox Theatre in partnership with the Municipal Opera Association. In 1982 Hal Dean,

CEO of Ralston Purina and the architect of the LaSalle Park redevelopment effort surrounding Ralston's corporate headquarters, retired from Ralston. Fr. Reinert prevailed on him to join CCRC as president, and subsequently Hal led the effort to sell $2,000,000 in 5% debentures to Civic Progress companies. This became the seed money necessary to begin in earnest the development of the district.

At this same time, the Board of CCRC was expanded to reflect the growth taking place within the district: Fr. Reinert, chairman; Hal Dean, president; Ian Chapman, Third Baptist Church; Bud Meissner, St. Louis Symphony Society; Leon Strauss, Harvey Harris, and Denny McDaniel, Fox; Al Kerth, Centerre; Walt Kaltwasser, Scottish Rite; Bob Frahm, Mercantile; Bill Douthit, Urban League, Lou Berra, consultant; Stanley Goodman, president, Grand Center Association. The highlight of CCRC's efforts was the celebration in September 1982, as the Fox Theatre reopened with a sell-out run of "Barnum."

Up until this time, all CCRC development had been enabled by liberal tax provisions—historic tax credit, real estate tax abatement, accelerated depreciation, UDAG financing, and the ability to utilize real estate losses to shelter other income. Utilizing these incentives, CCRC by 1986 had generated the investment of over $26,000,000 in the district. Some of the more noteworthy developments were: the State Office Building, Fox Theatre, parking lots with enough capacity to handle all of the venues anticipated, O'Donnell Building office equipment (formerly the Woolworth regional headquarters and originally the Saint Louis Club), University Club renovation into apartments, and Grand Center Park and the Goodman Fountain.

In 1985 the Board of CCRC asked Pantheon Corporation to assume responsibility for CCRC until resources could be found to continue the redevelopment effort. Richard Gaddes agreed to lead a renewed effort at development in Grand Center with the creation of Grand Center, Inc. Civic Progress endorsed the new Grand Center, Inc., and in 1988 the city of St. Louis agreed to undertake massive public improvements to the district with total commitment to approach $6 million.

Currently, though difficult economic conditions have slowed down developments in Grand Center, as has happened almost everywhere in inner cities, very encouraging developments are still in process. The Fox Theatre has invested heavily in expanding its capacity to attract outstanding shows by deepening its stage space. Both the Grandel Square Theatre and the Sheldon Concert Hall are expanding their offerings and audiences, and KETC-TV is poised to build a state-of-the-art television studio in Grand Center. Also, in the near future, ground breaking will take place for an art museum which will house the Pulitzer collection of modern art, one of the best in the world.

MIDTOWN MEDICAL CENTER REDEVELOPMENT CORP.

In the late 1970s, once organized efforts for the redevelopment and strengthening of the Midtown areas surrounding the University's Frost Campus were underway, Fr. Reinert turned his attention to the rehabilitation needs of the areas surrounding the University's Medical Center, including University-owned hospitals (Desloge and Wohl) as well as the immediately adjacent Cardinal Glennon, Bethesda, and Incarnate Word Hospitals. A redevelopment corporation called Midtown Medical Center Redevelopment Corporation (MMCRC) was established and was governed by a Board representative of the institutions named above, of several neighborhood organizations (e.g., Terry Park, Tiffany Gardens), and of major businesses located in the area. Working with city, state and federal agencies, plans for several redevelopment projects including townhouses and single family homes were projected. A unique plan to secure the financial support of Civic Progress corporations proposed that they demonstrate their interest in and support of prevention of blight in the inner city by authorizing the issuance of debenture bonds from company assets. A total of $842,000 was assembled which was added to funds from various governmental agencies to finance new and rehabilitated housing and business facilities. To the credit of the good faith and sincere concern of the leading businesses in St. Louis, these debenture obligations were nearly all forgiven, since it became evident in time that MMCRC would never become profitable enough to pay back its indebtedness.

Has MMCRC been a success? Yes and no. Yes, in the very true sense that if MMCRC had never been started, that large district would today be another "ghost town" very similar to Laclede Town. No, in the sense that the various housing projects have suffered from the almost universal experience of government-sponsored, "low-cost" efforts to provide decent, affordable housing for low to middle-income families: a) in today's market "affordable housing" for the poor is almost non-existent; b) exacerbating the problem of "red-lining" due to racial prejudice, it often happens that minorities disagree among themselves as to their desire for integrated or segregated neighborhoods; c) local residential communities often either cannot or will not exercise the leadership and discipline needed to prevent infiltration of drug dealers and other generators of crime, vandalism, etc.; d) overwhelming evidence demonstrates that government alone cannot provide the resources and stewardship necessary to create and maintain the basic necessities of community living. More enduring ways of empowering local communities to initiate and sustain the essentials of community life must be developed.

To work toward grassroots empowerment a new initiative in MMCRC has just been approved. The NHP Management Company has been engaged to assume the management responsibilities for the various MMCRC residential communities. Thorough investigation indicates that NHP is quite successful in managing, both equitably and efficiently, projects in several other cities with housing situations very similar to that of Midtown St. Louis. Future success will depend on the degree to which NHP can develop responsible leadership to promote and protect the resources of the local neighborhood communities.

Although there were and still are a substantial number of civic leaders and professional developers who have played a key role in guiding the University through difficult and frustrating negotiations with government, business, and individuals, special credit and thanks must go to Louis Berra, a graduate of Saint Louis University and currently president of Community Program Development Corporation.

CONFLUENCE ST. LOUIS

In 1982 a study was financed by the Danforth Foundation and the Monsanto Fund to formulate a proposal to form a citizens league that would supply an unbiased "voice for the entire St. Louis metropolitan community." The following year Confluence St. Louis was established. With a small staff and the help of hundreds of volunteer citizens, the primary role of Confluence is to identify the major issues facing the metropolitan area, e.g., housing, crime, transportation, etc. Extensive independent research is then applied to the issue under study, a volunteer committee of interested citizens is formed to examine the research data, to argue possible and/or feasible recommendations for change, and to eventually issue a report documenting the recommendations for community action. This report is then turned over to an "action" committee, which is charged with developing the best means and methods of implementing the recommendations.

In the late 1980s, Confluence chose to launch a major research study of the problem of racial tensions in the St. Louis area, and in 1989 the final task force report was issued "A New Spirit for St. Louis: Valuing Diversity," which outlined twelve major recommendations. Fr. Reinert agreed to serve as co-chair of the Implementation Committee, together with Kathryn Nelson, a program director at the Danforth Foundation and a highly respected educational and religious leader in the African American community. The Implementation Committee decided to initiate its action program by assembling forty-four community leaders in the areas of business, education, and religion as well as representatives of local government and community organizations. Since the conference was held in June 1990 at Fordyce House, Saint Louis University's conference center, it was designated the "Fordyce Two" Conference in view of the fact that a similar group of community leaders had assembled in 1969 as the first Fordyce Conference at the invitation of the Saint Louis University Center for Urban Programs and Metropolitan College. (This earlier conference had produced twenty recommendations dealing with racism, economic development, and needed changes in governmental structures, but since resources and manpower to followup were lacking, tangible results had not been forthcoming.) The Fordyce Two Conference was determined to set in motion committees that would work intensely on each of the twelve recommendations of the Confluence report.

Even a general summary of the efforts of the hundreds of committee members working on one of the committee recommendations would go far beyond the limitations of this chapter. Suffice it to say that Fr. Reinert feels, in retrospect, that the following are some of the major ongoing accomplishments of the "Valuing Our Diversity" community effort:

• Every member of the Fordyce Two Conference was required to write a "personal compact," in which, after thought, prayer, and consultation, each individual committed him/herself to a series of personal ongoing activities aimed at eliminating prejudice in their own attitudes and conduct. Most of the participants were willing to make their "compact" a matter of public record, and these are available in Confluence files.

- The business leaders who participated in Fordyce Two agreed to take the lead in establishing, within their own companies, a sophisticated prejudice reduction program. Such sensitivity training was initially to be a requirement for top executives and then eventually to extend downward through all administrative layers until every employee was educated. Two CEOs, Lee Liberman of Laclede Gas and Bill Cornelius of Union Electric, demonstrated superb leadership within their own companies and influenced other businesses to follow their example.

- The religious community responded by cooperating in a series of ecumenical programs and activities, e.g., the "Interfaith Convocation to Celebrate Diversity," which was held at Harris-Stowe State College in October 1991, and an extensive program of pulpit-exchanges involving ministers of all the major faith groups and various neighborhood gatherings of families affiliated with the many churches in the area.

- At the college and university level, an ongoing committee of student admissions and student life officers was formed and continues to meet, the chief topics of consideration being efforts to provide equal opportunity to all St. Louisans, regardless of race, as well as to offer counseling and whatever support needed for academic advancement.

SOME UNIQUE REWARDS FOR COMMUNITY SERVICE

Looking back over fifty years of community service, I treasure scores of friendships with so many remarkable St. Louisans, and I cannot resist recounting a few unforgettable experiences with these exceptional people which bolstered my Christian faith in Divine Providence's special interest in the healthy growth both of Saint Louis and of Saint Louis University.

FUND-RAISER FOR WASHINGTON UNIVERSITY

In 1958 in the process of organizing the University's first major capital campaign, Priority Needs, Joe Vatterott and the other volunteers had developed a strategy that $10 million of the total goal of $18 million should be sought from local corporations, and that the Monsanto Company should *be asked to make the lead corporate gift in the form of a 5-year pledge in the amount of $500,000—a huge increase over their current annual giving to the University. Furthermore, Joe Vatterott and Clint Whittemore were to set up an appointment with the formidable head of Monsanto, Edgar Queeny, at which time I would outline to Queeny the reasons why we mounted the campaign and why Monsanto should maintain its philanthropic leadership in St. Louis. After my explanation, Joe Vatterott would "ask for the order" —a $500,000 pledge. When we finally were granted a meeting with Edgar Queeny, I began my introductory remarks, only to be brusquely interrupted by Edgar: "I don't have time to listen to all this—I know why you're here: to ask for money. Well, you'll be happy to know that our contributions committee has already met and has decided to raise our annual contribution to Washington University and Saint Louis University so that each will receive $250,000 over a five-year period. I've already informed Ethan Shepley at Washington University, and he is very grateful." Edgar stared at the three of us, waiting for an enthusiastic "thank you"! I looked over at Joe Vatterott, and his loyal courage came to the fore: "Mr. Queeny, that's not enough!" Edgar flushed and snapped: "Joe, that's a hell of a lot of money!" Joe replied, "I didn't say it wasn't a big gift, but if you had listened to Fr. Reinert's presentation you would realize that unless Monsanto sets a level of $500,000, the proportionate gifts from other companies will cause us to fall far short of our goal. I'm sure you don't want to condemn us to failure!" Obviously very shaken, Queeny abruptly adjourned the meeting, and as we left his office, poor Joe said: "I guess I blew it."*

Several days later, Ethan Shepley called me and shouted over the phone: "Paul, you're the best friend Washington U. ever had!" "Ethan, what are you talking about?" "Edgar Queeny called me and said: Earlier I told you W.U. would be getting $250,000 over the next five years, but that damn Reinert and Vatterott won't take $250,000! So, I had another meeting of my committee, and you're both getting $500,000!"

MRS. HARRIET FORDYCE AND EXPANSION INTO THE MILL CREEK AREA

Early in my Presidency, members of our lay Board of Trustees, other friends, and benefactors urged me, in good faith, to consider moving the crowded, confined land-locked main campus out into the country. One possibility could have been the Chambers Farm in the Florissant area. The typical flight of people from the city's inner core was already in high gear—why shouldn't the University move out with them? My recollection is that not a single

Jesuit urged our moving, and I remember many a conversation in which it was pointed out that Ignatius himself always chose the inner city as sites for the Society's early schools, and faithful to that tradition, all of the Jesuit colleges and universities in the United States were definitely urban institutions.

Any doubt about the wisdom of staying where we were evaporated when Mayor Raymond Tucker announced that the city was to participate with HUD in the Mill Creek Urban Redevelopment Program, the single largest redevelopment project in the United States, stretching from Union Station westward to Grand Boulevard, about 460 acres. The amount of vacated land a not-for-profit institution could buy was limited; in our case we would be eligible to buy roughly 22 acres for $535,742. I can only credit supernatural intervention when we recalled that the property east of Grand Avenue was relatively close to the site of the battle of Camp Jackson, the incident where General Daniel Marsh Frost of the Confederate Army was captured in May 1861 by Captain (later to be named General) Nathaniel B. Lyon of the Union forces. Frost's daughter, Harriet Frost Fordyce, had often recalled how Fr. Peter DeSmet, in great favor with authorities in Washington because of his remarkably favorable relationships with the many Indian tribes scattered through the Midwest, was able to persuade Washington to have General Frost released from prison and restored to his St. Louis family on guarantee he would cease to participate in the Civil War. Accordingly, we alerted "Aunt Hattie" Fordyce of the University's once-in-a-lifetime opportunity to buy property close to the site of her father's capture. We suggested that we would place her father's name in perpetuity on both the existing campus west of Grand as well as the very large piece for expansion to the east side of Grand. Mrs. Fordyce promptly made arrangements for us to receive the money and Mayor Tucker was informed we were prepared to buy. But shortly after the sale was consummated, with no warning we were confronted with a lawsuit on the part of the Protestants and Other Americans United for the Separation of Church and State (POAU). Their argument was that the fair use value price we would be paying was somewhat less than if the property were bought on the open market and hence the differential would constitute a gift from the city to a not-for-profit religious organization. The University countered with the argument that by purchasing the property at a cost of between 55 and 60¢ per square foot, we would be paying a slightly higher rate for the property than other developers in the Mill Creek area. We won the case in the local courts; POAU appealed to the State Supreme Court in Jefferson City, the court decided to hear the case "en banc," and Saint Louis University finally won with five of the nine *judges voting in our favor. Thus, the question of moving out and ceasing to be "of, with, and for the city of St. Louis" was settled for the long future.*

Shortly thereafter another crisis arose: West Pine Street ran through our campus from west to east, but when it crossed Grand Avenue, it split into two streets, both of which continued down to the city—Pine and Lawton. In the triangle on the east side of Grand formed by the split into two streets stood a huge bronze statue of General Lyon on his horse. What a fiasco! It was bad enough that we were committed to placing the name of General Frost, the loser *on our expanded campus, but must we keep the statue of General Lyon, the* winner, *in the very heart of our Frost Campus? Once again, Mayor Tucker came to our rescue, and in the dead of night, city workers moved General Lyon to another triangle where streets converge just north of the Anheuser–Busch headquarters—one of the few "undercover" stories the "*Post-Dispatch*" has ever failed to discover and report!*

LIFE WITH GUSSIE BUSCH

The final two stories tell of some particularly memorable experiences in my close relationship with August (Gussie) Busch, Jr., a rough-hewn man who was basically good and generous at heart, but who never would allow even those closest to him to forget their obligation to acknowledge their dependence on him.

BUSCH MEMORIAL CENTER

*When at last all obstacles had been removed to our expansion across into the "Mill Creek" area east of Grand Avenue, we set to work planning the best use of this large area to meet the many physical needs of the University. One of the most obvious needs was for a replacement for Chouteau House which had been our first student union building, housing the offices of Student Life, "*The University News,*" ROTC, Dean of Students, etc. With the help of a government grant, we set about assembling funds to put up the first building east of Grand. Once again, Gussie Busch came to the rescue. I received a phone call from him in Tampa, Florida: "Father, our plant and gardens are completed and I am planning a dedication in the near future. I want the ceremony to begin with a blessing, and they tell me no minister in Florida will say a prayer over a brewery, so you have to come down here to do it." By that time, Gussie's wish was my command. So I flew down, said the prayer, and was conducted on a personal tour by Gussie himself. In the* *middle of the spacious gardens was a memorial plaque dedicating the new site to the three former chief executives of Anheuser-Busch—Gussie's grandfather, father, and brother. As I gazed at the impressive memorial, an inspiration struck me: "Gussie, where's the memorial to your predecessors in St. Louis where your company started? I want to talk to you about that." Thus was initiated the idea of the Busch Memorial Center, the first building to be erected on the new area east of Grand. It was largely financed by a contribution of Anheuser-Busch Company funds and money resulting from the company's "tax" on all of Anheuser-Busch's suppliers and distributors based on the number of barrels each was selling per year. Then, in the summer of 1963, through Senator Stuart Symington of Missouri, Gussie arranged for us to meet with President John Kennedy in order to invite him to attend ground-breaking for the Busch Memorial Center, scheduled for April 1964. The President agreed, but was assassinated in Texas in November 1963. President Lyndon Johnson agreed to honor his predecessor's commitment and came to St. Louis for the ceremony amidst the tightest security imaginable. The plaque honoring the first three founders of Anheuser-Busch is displayed in the lobby of the Center to which has been added an aluminum sculpture by Don Wiegand depicting a remarkable image of the fourth president of Anheuser-Busch, Gussie himself.*

THE CHAPEL, THE CARDINAL, AND THE COACH

The final story relates how two of my closest personal friends were brought together in their own bond of friendship—Cardinal Joseph Ritter and August Busch, Jr.

Gussie Busch was a man accustomed to getting what he wanted. Brash and even ruthless in his business dealings, he could nevertheless be generous and sentimental at unexpected moments, and often made sudden decisions that changed the lives of those around him. Traveling in Switzerland on business after World War II, Busch found himself in Lucerne, and inquired as to the best restaurant to get dinner. The answer, as he later was fond of relating, was the Swiss House, owned and operated by the Buholzer family. That night Gussie Busch was served dinner by one of the Buholzer daughters, Gertrude. With the suddenness and force of a kingly character in a fairy tale, Busch was smitten, and before long he had proposed to Gertrude, who was over twenty years his junior. She accepted on the condition that her marriage would be a valid one in the eyes of the Catholic Church. "Trudy" did make many trips back to her homeland, sometimes taking along her husband. After one such visit Busch called me and told me breathlessly, "Everybody (who's Catholic) who is anybody in Switzerland has his own chapel. I think it's a great idea and I want Trudy to have one too!" I explained that probably not every Catholic in Switzerland had his own chapel, and that in any case American bishops discouraged the practice, stressing instead the importance of membership and church attendance in a parish. Just recently, in fact, Cardinal Ritter, the Archbishop of Saint Louis, had ordered a family chapel closed. Busch was characteristically insistent, however, and I reluctantly agreed to go to Cardinal Ritter on behalf of my friend.

I fully expected the Cardinal to dismiss the idea of a Busch family chapel quickly, and even couched my request in terms that made it clear that a negative answer was expected. But the Cardinal was as capable of a surprise as was the brewer. Cardinal Ritter noted that Busch had been a friend of the Church, and that technically speaking, the erection of a Busch Chapel would not be providing the elder Busch with his own parish church, since he was not a Catholic anyway! No, His Eminence could see nothing wrong with such a project as long as it was made clear to Mr. Busch that it could not function as a parish church. Once given the go-ahead, Busch went to work making a clearing in the woods of Grant's Farm and importing materials from Switzerland for the chapel. Some months later, I again received a phone call from Busch. Again, he had a request. Could Cardinal Ritter come and bless the new chapel? I tried to explain to Busch that the Cardinal might be a little reluctant to come and endorse the opening of a family chapel when his official position had been to oppose them. Still, the beer magnate insisted. With even greater reluctance than before, I set out to visit the Cardinal. Once again, I prepared myself for a negative answer and once again the Cardinal surprised me, agreeing to bestow his blessing on the chapel.

On the appointed day the small company of Busch family members, Anheuser–Busch board members, and close friends gathered in the snow-shrouded woods of Grant's Farm. Cardinal Ritter arrived in a resplendent red robe, mitre, and cape, and was obviously pleased to be there. It would have been impossible for the prelate to have made his way through the snow, but Gussie Busch was nothing if not a problem-solver, and he had anticipated this difficulty. Waiting at the door of the Busch mansion was an electric golf cart which transported the Cardinal, crimson vestments flowing, through the woods to the chapel. Cardinal Ritter, for his part, then offered a blessing in English, a rarity in the days before Vatican II, which brought tears to the eyes of Gussie Busch. Following the ceremony the chapel's three bells, each one named for one of Gussie and Trudy's children, began to ring. The guests then returned to the Busch mansion where brunch was served, but the irrepressible Gussie had one more surprise. He asked Cardinal Ritter if he had ever driven in a coach-and-four. The cardinal replied that as a farm boy in Indiana he had ridden and driven horses in a variety of ways, but had never driven anything as elegant as a coach-and-four. "Then let's do it, your Eminence," Busch shouted, and within a few minutes the guests were treated to the sight of the Cardinal and Busch setting out on the snowy road driving the family coach-and-four. Those who saw it will never forget the Cardinal, obviously having a wonderful time, in full regalia, rounding a bend in the road. To this day I suspect that a group of tourists who caught sight of the crimson-clad coachmen thought they were just seeing one of the usual attractions at Grant's Farm.

The impetuosity, love of show, and determination that Gussie Busch exhibited on these occasions characterized his relations with the University. Like the scions of many American business dynasties, Gussie Busch was deeply influenced by both his heritage and his concerns for the perpetuation of the family concern. The Anheuser–Busch Brewery, when he took control of it, had already been a family business for three generations, and had weathered the difficult years of prohibition to become an industry giant. Gussie Busch endured many tragedies, such as the death of his five-year-old daughter Christina and his most unfortunate divorce from Gertrude Buholzer Busch in 1978, but each of these experiences nudged the hard-fisted man of business in the direction of seeking more stability and harmony in his life. One expression of this search was Busch's conversion to Catholicism. Related to and in some way parallel to Busch's commitment to Catholicism was his growing involvement with the University. For a man with no university education such a commitment might seem strange, but Saint Louis University became a haven where he could escape from the fierce competitiveness of the beer business; there he grew in admiration of men and women who were devoting their lives to the intellectual and moral education of young men and women. Most importantly, when he felt appreciated and respected, not for his tremendous wealth and the awesome power it gave him, but for his ever-growing generosity and self-giving on behalf of so many youth who could look forward to a successful, productive life largely because of the Busch Scholarship Endowment Fund.

Above: Francis and
Emma Reinert, Paul
Reinert's parents.
Right: Fr. Reinert's
parents and brother
on a delayed
"Honeymoon"
vacation in California

Right: Fr. Reinert as Dean of the College of Arts and Sciences, 1944-1948.
Left: The President of SLU entertains a visitor: his father. 1955. Photo
by Boleslaus T. Lukaszewski.

DuBourg Hall, home of the College of Arts and Sciences in the 1940s.

Reinert brothers and father. Back row: James, Paul, John;
front row: Francis and George.

Air view of the campus in 1948, showing the Quonset huts built to accommodate the postwar influx of students.

Air view of the campus about 1960, showing the Mill Creek expansion area east of Grand Boulevard.

Pius XII Memorial Library ground-breaking on June 3, 1957. From left:
Morton May, mayor Richard Tucker, Cardinal Ritter, Luke Hart,
Supreme Knight of the Knights of Columbus and Fr. Reinert.
Photo by Boleslaus T. Lukaszewski.

The laying of the cornerstone of the library, February 3, 1958:
Cardinal Ritter and Fr. Reinert. Photo by Boleslaus T. Lukaszewski.

Above: Ground-breaking of the Busch Memorial Center, with President Lyndon B. Johnson, February 14, 1964. Photo by T. Mike Fletcher. Right: Dedication of the Busch Center, with August ("Gussie") Busch, September 27, 1967. Photo by Boleslaus T. Lukaszewski.

Bob Hope receives the Spirit of Saint Louis Award from Fr. Reinert, 1968.

Fr. Reinert and alumni leaders in the Priority Needs Campaign, 1959–1963.

Fr. Reinert confronting anti-R.O.T.C. student protests in front of Chouteau House (now Cupples House), May 5, 1970.

Dr. Edward Doisy, third from left, surrounded by fellow Nobel Prize winners in the sciences, October 1965. Photo by T. Mike Fletcher.

Former President Gerald Ford presents Fr. Reinert with the Academy for Educational Development Award, May 18, 1977. Photo by Nate Silverstein.

Fr. Reinert receives the "Man of the Year" (1964) award from Richard Amberg, Managing Editor of the St. Louis *Globe-Democrat*. Photo by Boleslaus T. Lukaszewski.

Fr. Reinert in his office, greeting a visitor. Photo by Daniel T. Magidson.

Fr. Reinert and a young friend. Photo by Richard C. Finke.

Firmin Desloge Hospital, completed in 1932. Photo by Richard C. Finke.

Left: Fr. Walter J. Ong, S.J., University Professor of Humanities. Right: Fr. William Faherty, S.J., Professor of History. Photos by Boleslaus T. Lukaszewski.

Left: Fr. Alphonse M. Schwitalla, S.J., founder and first Dean of the School of Medicine. Right: Fr. Reinert with his Executive Vice President, Fr. Jerome J. Marchetti, S.J.

Ritter Hall, the new home of the College of Arts and Sciences, opened in 1967. Photo by Randy R. McGuire.

Dr. Kurt von Schuschnigg, former Chancellor of Austria, and Professor of Government at SLU for many years. Photo by Boleslaus T. Lukaszewski.

The expanded University Hospital.

Left: DuBourg Hall, built in 1888, and one of the campus gates, installed
in the 1990s. Photo by Elizabeth A. McGuire. Right: The new clock
tower, dedicated November 16, 1993.

St. Louis University administration, faculty, and alumni gather to celebrate fifty years of integration at the university, 1945–1995. Photo by Steve Dolan.

CHAPTER
SEVEN

JOURNEYINGS

TRAVEL TEACHES TOLERATION.

—DISRAELI

P aralleling the other ways in which the University grew in the decades after the war, the mobility and visibility of the president of the University also increased. Previous presidents of the University had ranged from reclusive to cautiously open in their dealings with the outside world. One president, Fr. Harry B. Crimmins, had resigned his office during the Second World War to serve as a military chaplain, but few had traveled widely during their tenures. Fr. Reinert broke with this tradition and became a globe-trotting president and later chancellor.

Two considerations brought about these journeys to distant, and significantly, predominantly non-Catholic lands. The first was the drive to make the University truly international in its vision and mission. Improvements in transportation and a worldwide trend in which the United States became the goal of thousands of international students, as well as the desire of American students to study abroad, encouraged the University to expand its international connections. Contacts with other nations could result in new sources of funding for the University, increase diversity in the student body, and provide new possibilities for teaching and research. Moreover, as other American colleges and universities established overseas programs and campuses, so did Saint Louis University.

An even more pointed reason for Fr. Reinert's journeys to remote corners of the globe were the needs of people in other lands. The end of colonialism and the rising expectations of the youth of many countries created a tremendous demand for American expertise and advice regarding the establishment of higher education programs. Many countries were eager to develop programs that would encourage their students to stay in their own homelands instead of coming to America to study. In other instances, such as El Salvador, the need was not for guidance in the running of a university, but for the moral credibility and the media attention that a respected educational leader could bring to a discussion of human rights abuses. Thus, Fr. Reinert often found himself called upon to play the role of representative, not merely of Saint Louis University, but of all American higher education and even of America itself. The following are brief accounts of a few of these undertakings.

SOUTH AFRICA, 1968

In 1968 the people of the Republic of South Africa had been subject to the policy of apartheid for twenty years. The institution of laws restricting contact between South Africans of European descent, called Afrikaners, and those of African, Asian, or mixed racial (Colored) ancestry had continued throughout the 1950s and '60s, culminating in a system of segregation that encompassed every facet of life, including education. Not only did the South African government perpetuate a separate and unequal legal relationship among the races, it also was slow to encourage the improvement of the environment in which its non-white citizens lived and worked. These environments ranged from squalid urban townships such as Soweto to impoverished rural areas in the north and west of the country, but the most characteristic development was the urban slum, which became increasingly common in the 1960s.

In the summer (or from the South African perspective, winter) of 1968, Fr. Reinert traveled for three weeks in South Africa as a participant in the "United States–South Africa Leader Exchange Program" sponsored by the Carnegie Corporation for the Advancement of Learning. His goal was to acquire a general understanding of the status of higher learning throughout South Africa and of the relationship of institutions of higher education to their surrounding communities. Specifically, Fr. Reinert sought to learn "what efforts these urban institutions were exerting to channel their academic resources in the direction of identifying, analyzing, and solving the problems arising from the urbanization process." He found higher education in South Africa to be in a state of considerable change, and the level of commitment of colleges and universities to addressing the problems of urbanization very uneven. Some schools seemed to take no interest at all in their surrounding communities, while others attempted, despite slender resources, to make an impact on the disadvantaged, particularly by developing the skills needed for employability.

Fr. Reinert had some difficulty obtaining a visa to South Africa. When he applied at the South African consulate, he was told that he had "three strikes" against him. First, he was an American, and Americans were unpopular with the South African government after the controversial visit of Senator Robert Kennedy, who had criticized the policy of apartheid. Second, he was a Roman Catholic, and the Catholic Church was an outspoken minority against the coalition of the South African government and the Dutch Reformed Church. And third, he was a Jesuit associated with a missionary order that currently was being advised to leave the country. Fr. Reinert was eventually granted a visa only after his reluctant consent to be accompanied by a secret service officer and to make no public statements outside of college or university campuses.

The South Africa which Fr. Reinert encountered was outwardly calm and smoothly functioning. The large cities presented a picture of cooperation and even contentment. In more intimate conversations, however, he became aware of the widespread tension among ethnic groups and between whites holding different opinions regarding apartheid. There were, in Fr. Reinert's opinion, significant parallels between the attitudes of many Afrikaners and white Americans with regard to the civil and economic rights of non-whites. Both dominant groups were living in a state of uneasy fear.

Fr. Reinert visited fourteen institutions, among them the University of Witwatersrand, the University of South Africa in Pretoria, the

University College for Indians at Durban, and Rhodes University, as well as several much smaller schools located in the remote back country. The diversity of size and resources among these schools was remarkable. The best equipped and most thoroughly integrated university in the Republic, the University of South Africa in Pretoria, boasted an enrollment of 21,000, a bilingual and multi-racial student body, and business programs, which, in the opinion of Fr. Reinert, compared favorably with those of the most elite American universities. By contrast, St. Bede's Anglican College at Umtata was a tiny facility training no more than thirty students for the ministry. In all institutions, the issue of racial inequality and segregation was either overtly or covertly an object of concern. This was made most clear during the first student sit-in in South Africa, which occurred while Fr. Reinert was visiting Capetown University. On this occasion about 300 students occupied rooms in the Administration Building in protest of the University's refusal to reappoint an African lecturer in cultural anthropology. Significantly, the protesting students received some support from their colleagues at English-language universities in the Republic, but virtually none from those universities with predominantly Afrikaner enrollments.

It was Fr. Reinert's assessment that while the Afrikaner government had invested millions of dollars in providing higher education institutions for the indigenous population in each "homeland," the system was doomed to more failures than successes. In Zululand, for example, an excellent facility with state-of-the-art scientific equipment had been erected. But first-rate faculty were not available, nor students who were both qualified and interested in pursuing preparation for careers not appropriate for the homeland in which these students were required by law to reside.

The "separate but equal" position of the Dutch Reformed Church, hitherto a bastion of Afrikaner nationalism, was being challenged by some of its own prominent members. However, this challenge was not entirely direct and frontal in nature. In a manner that was eerily reminiscent of conditions in St. Louis several decades earlier, church leaders in South Africa cited a mixture of Scriptural arguments and fears about social turmoil to justify their opposition to racial equality. At the same time opponents of apartheid within the Dutch Reformed Church used the pulpit or the professor's lectern occasionally to take on the status quo. In the late 1960s the outcome of this confrontation seemed in doubt, although the ruling whites possessed and employed both the machinery of government and the courts as well as the brute force of the South African military and its paramilitary partners to support the position of the Dutch Reformed Church regarding apartheid.

In retrospect, Fr. Reinert's visit to the then-isolated Republic of South Africa provided much information but few obvious answers to the problems of apartheid. The country presented itself as a set of contradictions: wealthy yet filled with poverty, seemingly peaceful but profoundly twisted by racial and ethnic divisions, a country where advanced research facilities were erected in desolate areas while urban Africans faced huge hurdles in obtaining a basic education. For so many white South Africans of that day, the notion of separate and unequal treatment of various groups seemed as self-evident and rational as it had to many Americans a few years before. Let us hope that for both nations, such attitudes are now becoming matters of history rather than current reality.

ISRAEL, JULY 8–22, 1970

During the 1950s and 1960s, in spite of continuing tension with neighboring countries as well as with Palestinians within its borders, Israel was forging ahead both educationally and industrially. Most of the capital for construction of the "new" universities was being furnished by Jewish Americans. By the summer of 1970 a concern was being expressed that possibly the multiplication of educational institutions was excessive and not properly oriented to the needs of the upcoming generations. This concern on the part of Jewish leaders in St. Louis, especially Melvin Dubinsky, a 1935 graduate of our Business School, generated a request for Fr. Reinert to spend as much time in Israel as he could afford in the summer of 1970, visiting the higher educational institutions and consulting with administrators, faculty and students. Fr. Reinert's only obligation in return for this fully-financed trip was willingness to give lectures upon his return, describing his impressions and evaluations based on his intensive but obviously somewhat superficial investigations.

Thanks to a tight, pre-arranged schedule of interview, and a guide totally at his disposal—Itzhak Tamir—Fr. Reinert visited the Hebrew University, Tel Aviv University, the new Technicon in Haifa, the University of Haifa, the new University of the Negev, Bar Ilan

University, Weismann Institute of Science, and also two ecumenical institutions: The Ecumenical Institute for Advanced Theological Study, and Hebrew Union College.

There were four major impressions which Fr. Reinert brought back from this whirlwind expedition, and these constituted the heart of the report that he brought back to the St. Louis Jewish community:

1. All of education in Israel was going through a painful evaluation and reform, motivated largely by a desire to develop social integration among young Israelis.

2. There was desperate need of national and regional planning and coordination to prevent the already serious duplication and competition. For example, Israel was already experiencing the same imbalance from which the United States has been suffering: too high a percentage of medical specialists clustered in major cities, too few deliverers of primary care in the smaller communities such as Caesarea.

3. The third observation deals with a thorny topic that cannot be thoroughly explored in the space available here: How can a democratic nation provide and support institutions of higher learning in which every citizen is provided an opportunity to explore *all* of human knowledge and history including religious studies, theology, ethics, etc.? In Israel, according to the Ministry of Education and Culture: "All accredited universities are independent both academically and administratively." As evidence of that, in 1970 each university was receiving 70% of its operating budget and 40% of its investment budget from public funds. Clearly, this is a totally different public policy than the one governing higher educational institutions in the United States. As Israeli higher education becomes more "democratic" and more international, it will be interesting to see whether the policies in force twenty-five years will persist.

4. Finally, Fr. Reinert could not help being deeply impressed with a philosophy of higher education which he frequently heard expressed by administration and faculty in the universities in Israel. To put it one way: Western man has always held fast to two

important articles of faith, that the individual is all-important and possesses a God-given dignity as his birthright, and that this dignity, together with reason, differentiates him from the rest of nature. But will this modern world of technology tolerate such a philosophy? In Israel, in the USA, in China, and across the globe, we need to heed the warning Lewis Mumford once issued:

"[The technology, the utilitarians, the computer slaves] forgot that the moral and intellectual traditions of Judaea, Greece, and Rome were essential to the development of the New World ideology itself: so that, with the ebbing away of this older tide of culture, the insufficiency of their own creed as a guide to life would become plain."[1]

These cultural–religious–educational struggles quite apparent in the "new" Israel I was visiting were made much more personal in my day-to-day contact and conversations with my wonderful guide, Itzhak Tamir—a self-made historian, sociologist, and as it turned out, something of a theologian as well. Itzhak had three children, all in the military at the time. The two sons were fighter pilots, the daughter was stationed at the Tel Aviv Airport. Every day as we drove to another University, our conversations, as I soon learned, must be punctuated by half-hour intervals so Itzhak could tune in on recent outbreaks of fighting.

One day Itzhak asked if I would like to visit Jacob's well. He warned it was in Nableth, "one of the worst towns in Israel," but "they know me—you'll be safe." As we approached the city's ancient walls, Itzhak stopped the car and pulled out a huge shotgun from the back seat and propped it up so it was visible between us in the front seat. We spent a few minutes at Jacob's Well and then Itzhak toured me through the same street where a few days before thugs on the street corner had stoned a bus-load of tourists. We visited an enclave occupied by a Nazarene sect where we saw many children suffering from birth defects resulting from this sect's prohibition of marriage outside the sect.

On the way back to Jerusalem, Itzhak asked me if I would be interested in hearing his theory on the origins of Christianity. I assured him I would indeed. Well, he said, Jesus had been a good man, a reforming rabbi who appeared at a point in the history of Judaism when the religion had become

---

[1]Lewis Mumford, *The Condition of Man*, 1944 (New York: Harcourt, 1973), p. 391.

corrupt and overly legalistic. By his teaching and his heroic willingness to die rather than compromise his religious principles, Jesus' powerful leadership might well have led to the reformation and revitalization of Judaism, "But something went wrong," Itzhak interjected, "that damn Paul came along reinterpreting Jesus' teachings so they applied it to Gentiles as well as Jews. That messed things up," he said, "and they were never the same again."

Truly a remarkable human being—"an Israelite in whom there is no deceit!" (John 1:47) Through the long years since 1970, we have continued to exchange holiday greetings.

IRAN, MAY 15–22, 1976

In the 1970s Iran was a nation undergoing a profound transformation. Led by the Shah Mohammed Reza Pahlavi, the country was introduced to an intensive program of modernization and Westernization. Traditional dress and Islamic law were in many cases supplanted by Western models of conduct. In particular, the officially encouraged attitudes toward big business, urbanization, educational reform, and development of the infrastructure reflected a clear desire for Iran to become a major modern world power. Supported by oil revenues, both public works projects and privately financed development began to change the face of the country.

At the same time, opposition to these changes was suppressed, often ruthlessly. The Shah's vision of a new Iran did not include democratic principles as understood in the West.   Censorship of the press, surveillance, harassment, and even violence against political and religious dissidents was common. The position of the United States relative to these developments was equivocal. American business interests were deeply involved in the Shah's plans, and they felt they stood to gain much by the continuance of his policies. Americans, whether they realized it or not, consumed billions of dollars worth of Iranian oil. Thousands of Iranian students attended American universities. American military advisors worked with the Shah, and American corporations sold his government military hardware. The Nixon and Ford Administrations viewed the Shah as an important ally in a volatile region of the world. Yet the dictatorial ways of the Shah's government, the suppression of dissidents, and the hikes in the price of Iranian oil were widely reported in the media, producing negative reactions among many Americans. The Shah was perhaps America's friend (as he often asserted), but a friend whose ways were not always understood or reliable.

In the spring of 1975 Ardeshir Zahedi, the Iranian Ambassador to Washington, contacted Fr. Reinert's office with a proposal. Ambassador Zahedi, a highly visible diplomat whose parties were known as the most lavish in Washington, was in the process of establishing contacts between American universities and his country's government. He had conducted research, he said, and had determined that the Saint Louis University School of Nursing would be the optimal institution to help establish a school of nursing in Teheran. Several visits to St. Louis and an exchange of correspondence followed, culminating in an invitation to Fr. Reinert, Dr. George F. Thoma, Vice President for the Saint Louis University Medical Center, and Mrs. Thoma to visit Iran to discuss more specifically plans for the establishment of a nursing school.

Fr. Reinert and the Thomas, therefore, embarked on a one-week trip to Iran in May of 1976. They flew to Teheran on the inaugural flight of Iran Airlines' 707 direct service from New York with a group of business figures and celebrities, including Elizabeth Taylor. This was no accident, for Fr. Reinert's visit had been timed to coincide with lavish celebrations marking the twenty-fifth anniversary of the Shah's reign. In fact, the entire tenor of the visit reflected the Iranian government's efforts to combine business connections, educational programs, and Hollywood glamour in its relationship with the United States. Fr. Reinert and the Thomas were given an official tour of the country, which quickly revealed that there were in fact two countries, Teheran and the surrounding countryside. While the skyscrapers and traffic jams of the capital city reflected the Shah's efforts to Westernize his nation, the rest of the country provided a striking contrast. Traditional dress and customs predominated, and while the visiting Americans were treated as honored guests of a successful and strong government, it was evident to them that there was serious opposition to the Shah's modernization program. The Americans also quickly discovered that the health education program which they were being asked to help set up was to be heavily influenced by the Royal Family and in competition with the existing system. It was also clear that the creation of educational institutions in Iran was intended to reverse the pattern of Iranian students studying overseas but not returning to aid their own country.

The Shah's wife, Queen Farah, was the most powerful proponent of the nursing school idea. Fr. Reinert recalled his conversations with the Queen as the most notable moment on his journey. Educated in European schools and rumored to be very sympathetic, if not an actual convert to, Christianity, the Queen believed that traditional interpretation of the Koran as practiced in Iran did not place sufficient emphasis on the helping professions and that the input of a Catholic medical program would be very beneficial. When she expressed this view to Fr. Reinert, she stressed that she saw the respect for the individual and the service mission of Jesuit education as great potential assets to Iran. Whether this opinion was shared by many outside the Royal Family's circle was less clear.

The formal relationship between the Iranian government and the University never progressed beyond this preliminary stage. Despite continued contacts between the Shah's government and the University, and a pro forma affiliation of the University with a consortium of American schools and businesses working with Iran, progress toward the creation of a nursing school was slow. By late 1978 the Shah's regime was in trouble. Fundamentalist backlash against Westernization and continued anger over political oppression and unequal distribution of wealth crystallized into an Islamic revolution led by the exiled Ayatollah Ruhollah Khomeini. The Shah fled his homeland on January 16, 1979, never to return. Western-style secular institutions were soon abolished, and Iran became one of the most completely theocratic societies in the world.

I was flattered by the invitation to visit Iran, and excited by the chance to contribute to the development of this country. While it was never certain that we would be able to establish the kind of nursing school envisioned by the Royal Family, and the chance remained that even if the Shah had stayed in power there might have been other difficulties, we still saw the connection as a wonderful opportunity to broaden the horizons and the mission of the University. What did I learn from this experience? Well, I had never visited a predominantly Islamic society before, and had little experience with countries having a state religion. I came away feeling even more strongly that institutionalized religion should not be run by the existing government. Choice in these matters is so important. We met many people who favored change in Iran, and saw conditions that suggested just how difficult, if not impossible, it would be to perpetuate those changes. Equal opportunity was still a slogan, not a reality, and I don't know when if ever it would have become reality. Even though there were few Christians in Iran, I felt that we could contribute much: Jesuits have been involved in the Westernization programs of non-Catholic countries since the days of Catherine the Great of Russia. We hoped for the best—but it was undoubtedly providential that we were thwarted in our well-intentioned "SLU in Iran" venture.

EL SALVADOR, JANUARY 3–10, 1983

For several decades there has existed a national network of American academics, headquartered in California, called FACHRES/CA, the Faculty for Human Rights in El Salvador and Central America. Many of the leading members of this organization are professors who formerly taught in their native Latin American educational institutions, but who had been exiled for "subversive" teaching or who came to America to escape the intolerable governmental and military oppression against "liberal" educators in El Salvador. The major mission of this organization has been to inform U.S. citizens, and especially those in positions of influence, of the bloody repression of Salvadoran proponents for democracy and protection of human rights. FACHRES/CA reasoned that if American educators would be willing to visit El Salvador and make as thorough an investigation as the government would allow, the evidence thus produced might provide a badly needed counter-balance to the "party line" reports being issued by the U.S. State Department. This was the origin of Fr. Reinert's invitation to join one such delegation composed of eight educators from a cross-section of American institutions.

A brief historical comment to place Fr. Reinert's visit in context: In the last year or two, with the ending of its civil war, El Salvador has slipped from the front pages of American newspapers and it is easy to forget the long years of suffering this small nation underwent not long ago. The early 1980s were witness to the murder of Archbishop Oscar Romero and hundreds of other Salvadorans at the hands of right-wing death squads. The position of the United States was fiercely debated; officially the American government supported the anti-Communist regime of Alvaro Magana, but many Americans deplored the continual violence and publicly aired their suspicion that American money and weapons were funding the murders of innocent civilians. Despite the Reagan Administration's insistence that support for Magana's government was necessary to prevent the advance of Communism, news reports continued to relate gross human rights violations on the part of both government forces and clandestine death squads.

Fr. Reinert spent a week in El Salvador, from January 5 to 12, 1983, as a participant in the FACHRES/CA fact-finding mission. The visit, although brief, included interviews with the major political players in El Salvador: U.S. Ambassador Dean Hinton, President Magana, former (and future) Salvadoran President José Napoleon Duarte, military leaders, educators, clergy, prisoners, and many others. Although the Salvadoran government went to considerable lengths to present its side of the story and was materially supported in its efforts by the United States Embassy, Fr. Reinert was confronted by images of a devastated land, paralyzed by violence.

Although the members of the FACHRES-CA mission had anticipated encountering evidence of human rights violations, nothing could have actually prepared them for the horrors they found in hospitals and refugee camps. Political prisoners showed acid burns on their bodies and told Fr. Reinert of being raped, subjected to electrical shock, and being suffocated with rubber hoods. The schools of El Salvador were revealed to be in a state of virtual collapse. One-third of the country's 2,700 schools were closed, and the National University maintained only a shadow existence in rented quarters. Visits to a men's and a women's prison revealed that nearly half of the inmates were political prisoners, and that a high percentage of them were teachers.

Underlying the abuse of El Salvador's educational institutions was the attitude of the regime that teaching itself was a subversive activity. Education of the peasant population was equated with deliberate attempts at political radicalization, the ultimate purpose being the overthrow of the existing government. Colonel Francisco A. Moran branded the publicity surrounding human rights abuses against teachers, clergy, and others as political propaganda against government officials. Colonel Moran, head of El Salvador's internal security forces known as the Hacienda, told the FACHRES-CA delegates: "We are totally professional; we respect human rights, what is said about us is mostly not true. . . . You must realize that 90% of the foreign papers are pro-Communist, that subversion is always guilty of lies and exploitation. . . . Unfortunately, education can produce negative effects. International Communism has infiltrated both education and the church."

Colonel Moran's fear of education and paranoia regarding

Communist infiltration became threateningly clear when he shook his finger in Fr. Reinert's face and told him that a priest, of all people, should know how evil Communism was and how it should be stopped by any measure necessary. The interviews and tours undertaken by the FACHRES-CA mission produced a consistent pattern: abundant evidence of flagrant human rights abuses, stonewalling denials by government officials, frequently laced with improbable details (i.e., U.S. Ambassador White had been drunk when he came to claim the bodies of American nuns murdered by death squads), and a seeming unawareness of actual conditions on the part of U.S. State Department officials.

As a Christian and as an American citizen, Fr. Reinert was deeply troubled by both the clear evidence of atrocities found everywhere in El Salvador and by the apparent acquiescence of American officials to these crimes. The precise degree of culpability of the United States was extremely difficult to determine with certainty: on the one hand was the laissez-faire position of a State Department official who said, "The law doesn't require us to certify that [the Salvadoran] government is perfect. What we have to certify is that they're making a concerted effort to end abuses." More disturbing was the statement of a girl who had been tortured with a machine which she said had been brought from America, and she reported that an American had given directions on how to operate the machine. There was abundant evidence that American financial support, even when intended for benign purposes, was being used chiefly to kill and injure innocent Salvadorans.

The final report of the eight educators, a copy of which was submitted to the U.S. Department of State stated: "Although we did not visit El Salvador specifically to monitor compliance for certification, we saw little evidence of government compliance with internationally recognized human rights. . . . We suggest the U.S. government consider allocating resources to the restoration of the National University. . . . We perceive the present situation of Salvadoran education at all levels to be symptomatic of the military domination of the country, and of the subordination of human rights and civil institutions to the government's war against 'subversion'."

Fr. Reinert's personal impressions and public stance on conditions in the Central American country thus were in opposition to the official position of his own country's government. More than this, by publicly taking sides on a foreign policy debate which was carried on in highly partisan terms, Fr. Reinert could not avoid having his own position viewed in terms of domestic American politics. The Reagan Administration's support for the government of El Salvador needs to be viewed in the context of a much broader campaign against Communism that included denunciations of the Soviet Union as the "evil empire" and the mining of Nicaraguan harbors. To challenge the anti-Communist stance of the Republican administration placed Fr. Reinert, the chancellor and chief fund-raiser for Saint Louis University, on the opposite side of a partisan controversy from some of the University's biggest donors. Nevertheless, the St. Louis press reportage of Fr. Reinert's visit and his comments critical of the Salvadoran government was favorable, and although the chancellor was later denied another visa to El Salvador, he received no explicit censure from the United States government.

The mission's public criticisms of human rights abuses in El Salvador came only four days before the deadline for President Reagan to recertify the Salvadoran government as eligible for continued military aid. In 1981 the U.S. Congress had forbade arms sales to El Salvador unless the President certified that the Salvadoran government was making "significant progress" in human rights and in controlling its armed forces. Despite criticism from some members of Congress, the Reagan Administration did certify that conditions in El Salvador were improving. Fr. Reinert's experiences in El Salvador and his responses to what he encountered there illustrate the dilemma which all members of a democracy face from time to time, and which those committed to education and justice feel most acutely. As chancellor of Saint Louis University, Fr. Reinert represented, and to a degree, interpreted, the University to a public of varying political views and social backgrounds. In this role, Fr. Reinert had to present a positive but generally non-controversial impression of the University. However, Fr. Reinert's responsibilities could not be bounded by his relationship to Saint Louis University. Paradoxically, the high degree of visibility which he achieved during his years as University president made him a likely candidate for the role of moral spokesman on matters of human rights. From his perspective, such a role was entirely compatible with his roles as educator and Jesuit. While a university president or chancellor must always make clear the distinction between his own personal opinion or conviction as contracted with the official positions of the institution itself, as a responsible citizen there are times when one must challenge claims of elected officials, and even enter into a controversy with strongly partisan overtones. Fr. Reinert believes that his nearly one hundred talks and debates subsequent to his return from El Salvador accomplished substantial good, even though it was necessary to contradict our government's claims. He summarized his position in these words: *"We ask what we can do when we go home? Make known what a travesty of justice is taking place. . . . The price that the United States is exacting in order to insure our own safety from a Communist takeover in El Salvador is the inhuman degradation of thousands of innocent people."*

Nineteen-eighty-three continued to be a year of horrors for El Salvador. Elections in April returned José Napoleon Duarte to the Presidency, but killings by right-wing death squads continued and 1,000 more civilians died by the year's end. The atrocities continued for six more years, reaching a particularly bitter climax, especially for Fr. Reinert and his Jesuit confreres at the University and elsewhere: on November 16, six Jesuits and two women (their cook and her daughter) were murdered in the courtyard of their residence at the University of Central America (UCA) in San Salvador.

UCA, of course, had been visited by the FACHRA-CA delegation in 1983, and was judged to be the most "open" institution in the country, training Salvadorans for careers in a wide array of professional fields undergirded with a strong commitment to social ethics and human rights. Outstanding on the faculty at UCA was Fr. John Sobrino, S.J., an alumnus of Saint Louis University, who was attending a conference out of the country and thus spared the bloody fate of his six Jesuit colleagues. As part of the Ignatian Anniversaries celebration in 1991, Father Sobrino gave one of the lecture series held in St. Francis Xavier (College) Church entitled "Rich and Poor Churches and the Compassion Principle." With his total involvement in the agonies of so many in El Salvador and other Third World countries, he was eminently qualified to challenge the U.S. and American perception of the world and its standards.

A weak economy and continued sabotage by guerrillas prevented the Salvadoran economy from making any significant gains during the next few years. By the early 1990s it seemed that both sides were at last growing tired of the killing. In January 1992 the government and the leaders of the guerrilla forces signed a comprehensive peace agreement, under whose terms the most important resistance movement, the Farabundo Martí National Liberation Front (FMLN), pledged to lay down its arms, and the government promised to enact land reform and other changes. The fate, however, of thousands of Salvadorans who "were disappeared" during the guerrilla war remained unknown.

REFLECTIONS ON "JOURNEYINGS"

As I reflect on my somewhat superficial encounter with the cultures of four countries vastly different from the United States, I am aware of a fundamental conflict that ebbs and flows in the emerging history of peoples of diverse origins, languages, and values. I can see more clearly that as a believer, a Christian, a Jesuit, I can share that faith effectively only, as our recent 34th General Congregation of Jesuits points out, ". . . through dialogue with members of other religious traditions, and through the engagement with culture which is essential for an effective presentation of the Gospel.[2] *. . . The dialogue between the Gospel and culture has to take place within the heart of the culture. It should be conducted among people who regard each other with respect, and who look together towards a shared human and social freedom."*[3]

I am also impressed with the fact that Jesuit higher education with the ultimate goal of nurturing men and women so that they develop into persons who are both more human and more divine, that academic centers such as Saint Louis University are the ideal medium, the most promising forum to provide the conditions which the 34th General Congregation suggests are essential if human society is to move toward enduring peace and justice for all:

1. *Effective dialogue with members of other traditions with a shared commitment to a transformation of cultural and social life.*

2. *Effective dialogue with the religions that inspire peoples, and an engagement with the social conditions that structure them.*

3. *'If our faith is directed towards God and His justice in the world, this justice cannot be achieved without, at the same time, attending to the cultural dimensions of social life. . .'*[4]

---

[2] Decrees of General Congregation 34 of the Society of Jesus (Rome: Curia of the Superior General, 1995), D 2, n. 40.

[3] *GC 34*, D 2, n. 42.

[4] *GC 34*, D 2, n. 46.

To prepare itself to embrace this as the primary comprehensive mission of Saint Louis University, the unification in each individual of a faith committed to peace and justice developed within his or her cultural heritage—that, I believe, is the major challenge to Saint Louis University in the century ahead.

CHAPTER
EIGHT

MEDICINE
AND
MORALITY

THESE ARE THE DAYS OF MIRACLES AND WONDER. . . .
MEDICINE IS MAGICAL AND MAGICAL IS ART.
THE BOY IN THE BUBBLE AND THE BABY WITH THE BABOON
HEART.

—PAUL SIMON, "THE BOY IN THE BUBBLE"

L ike most institutions in the United States, colleges and universities in America have grown and changed dramatically, particularly over the last half-century. In the case of Saint Louis University, our schools have multiplied: Parks College (1946), the School of Allied Health Professions (separated from the School of Nursing in 1979), the School of Business and Administration (from the School of Commerce and Finance in 1972), and the recently opened School of Public Health (1991). Some schools have closed: the decision

113

to close the School of Dentistry was made in 1967 (it became the Graduate School of Orthodontics) and in 1968 the Institute of Technology was closed (undergraduate engineering was discontinued, but strong departments in the earth sciences and meteorology were maintained). As president, Fr. Reinert necessarily was involved with the Trustees in the excruciating process of decision-making in each of these separate instances. But no school's development and periodic crises occupied more of his time and created more emotional tension than that of the School of Medicine, which stretched over most of the entire fifty years. We will detail only a few of the more traumatic episodes, since an in-depth history of our School of Medicine is being written by Dr. William Stoneman, the recently retired dean who is also an alumnus and has been closely identified with the School for fifty years.

When Fr. Reinert became president in 1949, all he knew about the School of Medicine was that it had been fathered and was still being magically orchestrated by a remarkable Jesuit, Fr. Alphonse M. Schwitalla. Earlier presidents of the University and high-level administration outside of his School knew little about the workings of Fr. Schwitalla's School. He was both feared and respected by faculty and students alike, and in medical and health education circles he was a national hero. But by 1948, at the age of 66, Fr. Schwitalla was clearly wearing out. This was so much the case that in January 1949, when Fr. Joseph Zuercher, the Provincial Superior at the time, informed Fr. Reinert that he would probably be appointed rector-president by the Superior General in Rome, he also added: "It's your job, but I strongly urge that the first two controversial decisions you should make immediately are: drop intercollegiate football, and find a replacement for Fr. Schwitalla in the Medical Center." And so began a fifty-year involvement with a series of traumatic changes in our School of Medicine. We will refer to only a sampling.

In 1953 Dr. James Colbert, a young, dynamic, ambitious academic administrator, was appointed dean. He shortly announced that he found the School in "a state of grave educational crisis," and laid out a major development plan centered on three elements: a full-time faculty, the creation of a University teaching and research hospital center, and a greatly expanded research activity. A year later, in 1954, Dr. Philip A. Tumulty, who held the key position of director of internal medicine, resigned, claiming he had not been given adequate funding nor control

over the teaching hospital beds in Firmin Desloge Hospital.[1]   Dr.
Colbert's unpredictable decisions climaxed in the sending out of a letter
in October 1961, in which he fired 149 volunteer, part-time faculty,
many of them Saint Louis University graduates, on the grounds that
they had not performed teaching assignments and were not referring
their patients to Firmin Desloge Hospital. The resulting intense internal
and external pressures were such that no resolution of the problems was
possible without the removal of Dr. Colbert as of December 31, 1961.

Fr. Jerome J. Marchetti, S.J., Executive Vice President and Fr.
Reinert's strong right arm in those difficult days, agreed with him that
they would have to find an interim dean who understood all the
intricacies of this problem involving the careers of the personnel not
only in the Schools of Medicine and Nursing but Desloge Hospital, as
well as the newer hospitals—Cardinal Glennon Hospital for Children
and Wohl Mental Health Institute. They asked Dr. Goronwy Broun,
Sr., a highly respected faculty member and former director of internal
medicine, to assume responsibility until such time as a competent
younger person could be put in charge. Out of his deep sense of loyalty,
Dr. Broun agreed to serve on condition that Fr. Reinert establish an
office next to his on the Medical Center campus and lend the President's
authority to whatever reorganization seemed necessary. From January
1962 to September 1964, Dr. Broun led the Medical Center out of chaos
and laid the groundwork for Dr. Robert Felix, former Director of the
National Institutes for Mental Health, to assume the deanship. With the
help of Fr. Ed Drummond, S.J., the first Vice President for the Medical
Center, he developed a long-range plan that systematically moved our
entire teaching, research, and health care system to a high level of quality
achievement.

Since those hectic days in the '50s and early '60s, I have often reflected on
the lessons I learned about the unique responsibilities and relationships which
a modern American university must assume in respect to its school of
medicine and related academic units. While at first glance the responsibility

---

[1] Completed in 1933, the Firmin Desloge Hospital served as the chief teaching center
of the School of Medicine until 1988 when the more modern Saint Louis University
Hospital was erected immediately west of Desloge. The former Firmin Desloge
Hospital became the Desloge Towers, which houses doctors' offices and research
facilities.

of training physicians and other health care professionals bears a resemblance to the job of training professionals in other fields, medicine is in a league by itself. No other undertaking of a modern university is so expensive, so freighted with moral and ethical dilemmas, and so closely tied to the deepest concerns of everyday people. And no facet of a university is more vulnerable to shifts in government policies regarding funding. The University Medical School, once a crucial but still generally manageable and comprehensible part of the University community, long ago evolved into a world of its own. Now as the new century approaches, the rules that have governed this world are changing beyond recognition.

The basic principles that have guided the practice of medicine since the time of Hippocrates have stressed the alleviation of suffering and the prolonging of life. But there have always been limits to what aid medicine could provide toward these ends. The contemporary medical school finds itself confronted with rapidly increasing potential to develop procedures that can prolong life. But even more important than the material advances themselves are the ethical questions of how far efforts should be made to prolong life. Americans, it may fairly be said, are preoccupied with the ideal of immortality. We simply want to go on forever. Considering the equally significant American obsession with immediate gratification, this uncritical desire to see the prolonging of life as an undiluted good seems a curious contradiction, but it is nevertheless a dominant theme in modern American medicine. American medical schools—and particularly—those claiming a Catholic identity—must come to terms with the limits of their responsibilities in this area. They must also be willing to explore the deeper question of why our culture is so concerned with extending life, and how the quantity *of this life may be measured against its* quality. *Theologians have long struggled with these questions; graduates of medical schools and other health science programs must become more conversant with both the shaping and the communicating of the issues at stake. For this to happen the Medical School must grow in terms of curriculum, pedagogy, and even fundamental institutional goals. The processes of specialization and mechanization of medicine, underway for the last two hundred years, must be undergirded by a holistic view of the body and the spirit.*

I am one of many who worry that the increasing predominance of materialistic and self-indulgent materialism as the be-all and end-all of life in the U.S. has effectively replaced the spiritual and humanistic values without which no truly free and just society can exist. One of the most frightening evidences of this deterioration is to be found in the evolution of health care in this nation. At bottom, it is an excessively materialistic,

*acquisitive society which is trying to place an impossible burden on the men
and women who wish to serve in the health care sciences.*

*Let me expand a bit on the dilemmas facing a school of medicine,
particularly a private one, as it strives to fulfill its mission in such turbulent
circumstances. First, in its hospital facilities it must provide the environment
where patients and their families receive the information that helps them to
make decisions about their own health care. Second, the medical school must
train, and it may be hoped, educate the health care professionals who provide
this information and who set the cultural and moral tone of the institutions
in which these momentous decisions are made. Third, the medical school
must engage in research that makes the lengthening of life possible.*

*With limited resources, a medical school must decide what portion of its
budget can be devoted to primary research, and what parts should be spent
on health education of the community, on preventive medicine, and on the
special training of medical professionals we have just alluded to. These
decisions of course do not occur in a political vacuum. Pharmaceutical
companies, medical societies, patient advocacy groups, politicians, insurance
companies, accrediting bodies, and many other forces seek to influence the
policy decisions of a medical school.*

*Another question pressing the contemporary American medical school
is the dilemma of research versus service. In other disciplines this dichotomy
may seem less urgent, but in medical education, especially when the school is
located in an urban environment, the question of responsibility is
unavoidable. American cities are filled with a seemingly endless number of
indigent and homeless people whose medical needs may not require state-of-
the-art medicine but who are shut out of basic health care as effectively as if
they required some as yet undiscovered medical breakthrough. Historically,
the Saint Louis University School of Medicine has endeavored to serve
individuals who have little access to other medical facilities in the city. The
cost of such service was never negligible, but today it threatens the financial
security of the school. The costs of even basic medical services have
consistently outpaced inflation and the expected revenues of a medical school.*

To summarize, in earlier days, we Americans traditionally
recognized a rather sharp distinction between the "business" or
"capitalistic" professions and the humane, less acquisitive professions of
ministry, education, law, and medicine. But in the last half-century that
distinction has become blurred if not eliminated. Lawyers seek business
in the same way as automobile salespersons, and the entire field of health
care delivery has become one of fierce financial competitiveness. One

of the many tragic consequences of this nationwide commercialization of health care delivery is the fact that the not-for-profit institutions which are essential participants in this extremely complicated process inevitably become the forgotten fall-out in the entrepreneurial process.

SLU CARE

At the risk of over-simplifying an extremely complicated situation, it might be helpful to try to explain the essentials of the revised system whereby the Health Sciences Center of Saint Louis University will conduct its two distinct businesses: 1) health professions education and 2) research and health services delivery. The first "business," health professions education, is the primary responsibility of the four health sciences schools—Medicine, Nursing, Allied Health, and Public Health. The second "business" is concerned with research and health service delivery. This second "business" is quite different from the academic health sciences educational enterprise. The clinical enterprise, consisting of the hospital and medical practice of the faculty, provides service in ambulatory and institutional settings and generates income from the provision of these services. Hence it competes in a market with private practitioners and community hospitals, a market which has become extremely competitive today.

In order to survive in today's health services market, the University's Health Sciences Center has established some new entities: a) in 1993 the University Medical Group (UMG), a group practice within the Health Sciences Center faculty, was created; and b) in 1995 SLU Care was authorized by the University Trustees as a single provider organization at the Health Sciences Center, an operating division of the University which will market and manage the clinical enterprise. SLU Care will be aggressively promoted in the St. Louis market and every effort will be made to establish relationships with other providers of health care in order to sustain an adequate referral base for Health Sciences Center tertiary care services. At the same time, an SLU Care primary physician network must be expanded. It should be pointed out that from the viewpoint of physical facilities on the Health Sciences Center campus, the SLU Care enterprise applies only to University-owned facilities: the academic and research buildings, University Hospital, Doctors' Office Building, Wohl, and Anheuser–Busch Eye Institute. The future status of affiliated hospitals, such as Cardinal

Glennon Hospital for Children and Bethesda Hospital, will be determined by their own Boards of Trustees independently of the University.

CHANGES IN THE SCHOOL OF MEDICINE

While the changes directly affecting health care delivery in hospitals, clinics, etc., directly impact on the general public and hence receive more attention and media coverage, it would seem important to conclude this chapter on the University's past and current experience in the field of medicine with a brief outline of the less obvious but equally dramatic changes in medical education, specifically of the young doctors who will be moving into a rapidly changing field in the immediate future.

In 1995 the School of Medicine embarked upon a renewal of its curriculum for medical students. This involved changes in curriculum governance, curriculum content, evaluation, educational strategies, and faculty development.

The last major curriculum reform at Saint Louis University School of Medicine took place in the late 1960s, when behavioral sciences were greatly expanded in the first two years of the curriculum. Since then, the instructional program has undergone gradual development and refinement, as it has been adapted to faculty and students' interests and needs.

Some of these changes include the addition of new courses (Medical Communication Skills, Death and Dying, Human Sexuality, Nutrition, and integrated Neurosciences); new methodologies (case-based learning in Physiology, Pharmacology, and Microbiology; videotaping, computers, standardized patients and teaching associates); new facilities (Clinical Skills Center, Educational Media Department); and new scheduling, such as the flexible Year 4 and reduction of lecture hours.

Although these and other innovations have contributed to a curriculum that appears to produce competent physicians, the progress achieved has not been sufficient to resolve the limitations inherent in a traditional, lecture-based curriculum.

It is important to have a renewed curriculum that coordinates and integrates the basic and clinical sciences throughout all four years. The curriculum must be one that will encourage the faculty to apply innovative approaches to teaching and evaluation and to select the most appropriate content and educational strategies. The curriculum will be suited to the needs of students to acquire the skills and knowledge needed to practice medicine competently and to develop the capacity for life-long learning; it must be one in which the students are active participants in the learning process, not passive recipients of facts learned in isolation from patient care. Computers and other emerging educational technologies must be an integral part of the curriculum that enhance the more traditional lectures, laboratories, and small-group activities.

Curriculum renewal poses a challenge for the faculty. The school is committed to providing the resources necessary to support this effort. Beyond the resources, the Faculty Affairs Committee has been asked to devise mechanisms to promote greater recognition for teaching to show support for the contributions of the faculty to the educational mission of the School of Medicine. This is the basis for curriculum renewal and change. The key to the success of these efforts is a spirit of cooperation and collaboration among all the departments of the School of Medicine.

While only time will tell whether this courageous reorganization of the University's mission in the fields of health sciences and health care is the most appropriate system to grapple with the critical problems faced by a private medical school today in achieving both academic and financial integrity, certainly it must be a more acceptable solution than the alternative of allowing a private university's health care delivery system to become entangled in the "dog-eat-dog" health care struggle so rampant especially in our major metropolitan areas.

My hope is that as the University, and especially the Health Sciences Center, goes through a tortuous metamorphosis, there will emerge educational programs in all the health science fields that will produce substantially more young men and women who are eager to provide holistic primary medical care to individuals, to families in smaller towns and villages, as well as in the most needy areas of our own American cities. I pray that more young men and women will come to our health care schools, not primarily because they seek a professional career that promises large monetary rewards, but because they are committed, as our Health Sciences Center is committed, "To the Glory of God and the Health of His People."

CHAPTER
NINE

VALUES

*EVERY SCIENCE AND EVERY INQUIRY, AND SIMILARLY EVERY
ACTIVITY AND PURSUIT, IS THOUGHT TO AIM AT SOME GOOD.*

—ARISTOTLE, NICOMACHEAN ETHICS

It is an ironic truth that the more successful and established an institution becomes, the easier it is for members of that institution to dodge issues of accountability. This is particularly true of educational enterprises. When Socrates was accused of corrupting the youth of Athens with his open-air discussions, there was no curriculum committee or department chair on which he could blame his dilemma. The hemlock was for him alone. As schools grow in size, reputation, and wealth (and sometimes arrogance), it becomes easier for all concerned to pass the buck. For a long time the new and often small American Jesuit universities did not have the luxury of worrying about avoidance of accountability. Today, however, the very success of institutions such as Saint Louis University makes the maintenance of a culture that promotes accountability a greater challenge. Today the temptations and the risks are greater, yet the need for the institution and

121

its members to be answerable for their actions is as basic as ever.

I believe accountability is and must be a foundation stone in the governance of a college or university, more so today than ever before. Fifty years ago when I was extremely active with the North Central Association of Colleges and Secondary Schools, the quality and integrity of a college or university was largely judged by quantitative criteria established by the Association: number of books in the library, median faculty salaries, number of faculty with terminal degrees, etc. Fortunately, we were able to shift from these artificial, quantitative measures to an evaluative process based on the insistence that each institution develop its own "Mission Statement," with the understanding that the examiners would judge each facet of the institution's operation as to the extent that the self-defined mission was indeed being achieved. This was a particularly important breakthrough for church-related and specifically Catholic institutions. Far from apologizing for educational objectives that included "character foundation," for example, the quality of our institutions could be measured, at least in part, by the success we were achieving in the formation of our students in the light of Judeo-Christian values.

Accountability extends beyond the impersonal institution called the university to members of the university community. Students and faculty must understand and be provided with the means to respond to the demands of accountability. This is somewhat more complicated than it might seem at first glance. Faculty find themselves pulled different ways by their multiple roles as teachers, mentors, conveyers of knowledge, researchers, and recognized experts communicating with the community on issues in their field. Each one of these roles arguably has its own sphere of accountability, and there is always the potential for conflict. This is where the university (meaning its administration, and in particular, it chief executive officer and trustees) must clarify the priorities of the institution so that faculty know precisely for what they are to be held accountable and to whom. While this may seem simply another onerous task for the already overworked administrator, careful attention to clarification of the roles of faculty will avoid many headaches later on.

Students need to understand in what way they too are held accountable. The experience of many students in public and private schools does not adequately stress ownership of their decisions or the reality that adults are held accountable for their actions and positions.

Too often the late assignment can be compensated by the hastily assembled extra credit project, the mediocre effort is considered adequate, and the sometimes uninspiring attitudes of hard-pressed teachers underscore the general sense that none of it really matters that much. The root causes of this culture of non-accountability are complex, and it is not our purpose to indict the public schools yet once more for their failure to produce the ideal graduating senior. Nevertheless, colleges and universities must deal with these graduating seniors. The worst thing that can happen to an incoming freshman is for these values (or, perhaps more accurately, the absence of values) to be reinforced by a collegiate culture that has few bottom lines, ethical, academic, or personal. This is a matter for more than just the professor in the lecture hall or seminar; it must be a concern for residence hall directors, campus ministry, coaches, tutors, and anyone else who comes in contact with the student.

Holding students accountable has an added advantage in that it promotes a "from the bottom up" culture of accountability spreading to instructors and, it is hoped, administrators. Such a culture can only take hold, however, if it is simultaneously supported by "top down" administrative positions. The interplay of these two complementary positions promotes the integrity of the university and its mission. We now turn to the problem of the challenges to this integrity.

Many of the challenges facing American universities in the next century are obvious to even a casual observer. Finding adequate funding, for example, will always be a major occupation for most not-for-profit educational institutions. There is another perennial challenge, however, which is less apparent to many friends of higher education. This is the challenge of maintaining institutional integrity and autonomy and sustaining the culture of the university while continuing to have meaningful connections with the outside world. Over the years, the struggle to remain independent has taken varying forms. In the High Middle Ages, the masters of universities clashed occasionally with the universities' founders—princes and prelates—over the exercise of institutional privileges. Just as often, masters and students engaged in "town and gown" riots with their neighbors. More recently, some American colleges and universities have come into conflict with sectarian dominated governing boards, or less often, with founders or donors whose vision of higher education differed from that of the faculty and administration.

Today, despite the occasional headline-grabbing actions of a few donors or administrators, the greatest challenge to institutional autonomy comes not from individuals, but from the demands of the educational marketplace. When medieval students brawled with townsfolk, the conflict was derived from differing value systems. The good burghers of the cities where medieval universities were located often viewed the young scholars as roisters who drank too much and conversed arrogantly in Latin, an unintelligible tongue associated with the elite professions of the Church and law. For their part, students too often haughtily regarded townspeople as unlettered boors. Yet, both groups were bound together by economics: the university and its members purchased goods, services, and real estate from the burghers, who in turn provided the university with some of its students and profited from the privilege and visibility which the university conferred on a town.

The current confrontation involves not town and gown rivalries of old, but the conflicting notion of what services a university should provide, and what the relationship of the student to the university should be. Formerly, these questions, at least in theory, were more clearly resolved. Half a century ago Saint Louis University drew its undergraduate student body heavily from the Jesuit and Catholic parochial schools of the St. Louis metropolitan area. Not only did this ensure a considerable degree of consistency in the type of academic presentation and religious training which freshmen would bring with them to the University, but it also assured that the perceptions of faculty and students as to the purpose and nature of education would be very compatible. We have already touched upon many of the challenges which have come to the University during the past fifty years: increased numbers of students from educational backgrounds other than Jesuit or Catholic parochial schools, the flood of female students, and the racial integration of the University, among others. Paralleling and in some cases accelerated by these developments has been a nationwide shift in the metaphor employed by students, administrators, and sometimes teachers to describe higher education. Whereas the relationship between teacher and student has been compared to that of master and disciple, craftsman and apprentice, or even parent and offspring, the new metaphor speaks of the student as a "customer" or "consumer" of a product or service provided by the university.

This development can only be described as momentous and differs from the relationship that has traditionally existed between teacher and student, or even between school and business. When students and tavern owners squabbled over the bill in fourteenth-century Paris, both sides regarded the university's business as qualitatively different from that of an innkeeper or silversmith. The current employment of a metaphor borrowed from the world of business points to a profound change in the perceived rights and responsibilities of student, teacher, and administrator. Implicit in the twentieth-century capitalist understanding of the consumer is the right, even the obligation, to "shop around" for the best deal for one's money. Equally implied in this concept is the right to question the product purchased if it does not meet with the customer's expectations. This consumerist attitude, which is increasingly employed in the American public's dealings with professionals in fields such as law and medicine, is undoubtedly beneficial in many ways. It has encouraged consumers to become better educated about the services they seek, and has impelled professionals to police their own ranks. These benefits extend to many areas of higher education. Students enrolled in a program leading to state certification or licensure have every right to ask for evidence that training in the program they have paid for will cover the appropriate material. Literal and immediate accountability is a legitimate facet of any discussion of the goals of higher education.

Yet, higher education, and we believe, Jesuit higher education in particular, is concerned with more than the immediate. In Chapter Eleven we will make a case for the importance of providing role models to both undergraduate and graduate students. Not only is a role model a difficult thing to define precisely, it is also an entity that does not adapt readily into a system driven by concerns for consumer satisfaction. Consider the following description by heart surgeon Dr. Michael DeBakey of a revered mentor: "He was all that I imagined a doctor ought to be. He set a very high standard for us. Yet he never lost that common touch."[1] To call such a statement "an endorsement from a satisfied customer" seems at the very least a vulgar trivialization. While recognizing that certain minimum standards must be met to meet the perceived demands of the marketplace, we should aim much higher than merely satisfying the consumer.

---

[1] Quoted in *Parade*, 20 November 1994, p. 11.

Nor would it be so simple to satisfy the "consumer" of a university education, even if we were to decide that this should be our primary goal. First, who *is* the consumer? Is it the student, swamped by the approach of finals, filling out a standardized course evaluation form? Is it this same student, reflecting on his or her education at graduation? Or is it the alumnus, years or decades removed from the collegiate experience, who finally realizes the benefits gained so many years before? The alumni and alumnae of Saint Louis University have spoken frequently and emphatically about the remarkable, life-changing experience their university education was. But how does an institution utilize these "endorsements" to market itself amidst other aggressive four-year colleges who may be operating in a time frame stressing a quick payoff of one's investment? Then, too, this short list of "consumers" leaves off several of the most important players in modern higher education: parents, who contribute to the cost of education; the Federal Government, which underwrites, directly or indirectly, the costs of millions of students; and employers, who encounter the "product" of higher education, the students. In a broader sense, the entire society in which university students will live their lives can also be regarded as a "consumer" with claims on the university which trains these students.

Before we leave this discussion of values as they relate specifically to students, Fr. Reinert wishes to emphasize a point that he feels is most pertinent:

Looking back over the past fifty years of academic growth at the University, I feel a very special sense of pride in the recent establishment on campus of a Billiken Hall of Fame and History. This is no ordinary collection of trophies—banners, plaques, and loving cups—dramatizing the University's success especially in intercollegiate basketball and soccer. Side by side on the walls of this Hall of Fame are both the athletic achievements of substantial numbers of our athletes and the equally impressive academic records of these same athletes. To mention only two: Richard Boushka, an all-American basketball star, who graduated from our Institute of Technology with a strong B+ four-year average; and "Easy Ed" Macauley, also an all-American basketball player (later a star for the Boston Celtics) who graduated from our College of Arts and Sciences with a B- four-year average. More importantly, Dick and Ed are not two unusual examples of combined academic and athletic excellence. The National Collegiate Athletic Association (NCAA) reports that since 1985 82% of our athletes competing in major sports have graduated. As a matter of fact, among NCAA universities, Saint Louis University ranks ninth in the entire country in the percentage of athletes who graduate from the University.

We now turn to the question of the product itself. There cannot be a consumer without something to consume, but the shift to a consumerist paradigm creates confusion as to what that product is. Some things with which a student leaves the university are extremely tangible: a diploma, a certification in a particular field, a grade point average, even a letter of recommendation. Yet taking these to be the most important products of a university education leaves the most important pieces missing. Again, an institution which claims to provide such intangibles as spiritual grounding, moral education, a sense of purpose, and models of what it is to be an adult, is not easily adaptable to an environment that stresses the goal-oriented, satisfied consumer. Yet, the university has never had the luxury of declaring that its mission has no relation to the world of consumer and product. That world is here, and it is populated with colleges and universities who promise prospective students fast-track and high-powered business careers, academic credit for "life experience," and a seemingly value-free curriculum.

In a real sense, an institution such as Saint Louis University cannot and should not compete with schools for "customers" who truly want what these institutions offer. But the other side of the coin is that Saint Louis University, and every other Catholic college and university, needs to consider why this shift in the perceptions of prospective students has taken place. Even if Jesuit institutions decided to "write off" the students who seem destined for schools with a more quick-fix appeal, there would still remain the question of this trend spreading to other segments of the school population, including those which Jesuit schools have traditionally looked to as good places for recruitment. More importantly, the philosophical difference between the Jesuit vision of higher education and the idea held by students attracted to other, more pragmatically oriented institutions should be extensively and publicly explored. If, in a market that exerts constant pressure on universities and colleges to opt for the main chance, Jesuit institutions choose to stand somewhat apart from the trend to view the diploma (and the implied job opportunity) as the ultimate product of higher education, they must articulate convincingly why they do so and how they achieve what they are striving for.

While Jesuit higher education strives to articulate its position, it must come to terms with the way its own prospective student body is changing. The easiest (and least useful) response is to decry the supposed intellectual and moral shallowness of popular culture, the triumph of relativism among contemporary college students, their lack of intellectual curiosity and their lack of stamina. In reality, students entering undergraduate studies are different from their parents or grandparents only partially because of changes in culture or school curricula. The principal difference between college freshmen of today and those of a few decades ago derives from their family experience.

Let us now consider the relationship of the university to the development of values, and how the family relates to both. However, we pause before we place the words "family" and "values" next to each other on the printed page. The phrase "family values" has become freighted with political and ideological significance, a shibboleth that sets liberals apart from conservatives, and sometimes, men apart from women. We do not intend to use these words in this way, or to exclude or condemn, but only to describe forces that have an impact. There are many kinds of families in the United States. Some are immigrant and some have roots reaching back centuries. Some are Catholic, some Jewish, some Buddhist, and some have no articulated religious faith but believe strongly in fairness, honesty, and hard work.

The American family has changed significantly in recent decades. This is a generalization encompassing many varying events that have affected different families in different ways. In general, American families are smaller than they were a generation or two ago. There is a much greater probability that both parents will work outside the home, and an increasing probability that there will be only one parent at home. These trends have been more visible in some socio-economic contexts than others, but have been evident throughout the nation. More than a few commentators have described the sum of these changes as a "decline" or a "crisis" for the family. Clearly what has happened is of great moment and is not generally perceived as an improvement.[2] The

---

[2] Some commentators trace the tension between the family and the American desire for independence back many decades before the apparent contemporary breakdown of the family. See Robert Bellah et al., *Habits of the Mind* (New York: Harper and

transformation of the family also has unmistakable implications for the university, to which we will now turn.

First there is the phenomenon of fragmentation. Not only is the extended family of a generation or two ago replaced by the nuclear family or the "subatomic" family unit, but the rhythms and patterns of family life are interrupted by the exigencies of a multiple income, multiple schedule lifestyle. Families regroup, move, or dissolve, placing their members, particularly children, in a state of continual reaction to crisis. Students are therefore often denied the chance to see long-term undertakings brought to completion. This is more significant than it might seem. One of the avowed goals of Jesuit higher education (and that of many other university traditions as well) is to promote the notion of lifelong commitment to personal relationships, moral positions, and intellectual undertakings. Undergraduates for whom these ideas are unfamiliar will find the increasingly self-motivated and maintained requirements of the university curriculum beyond their capabilities or decisions. Faced with students who cannot handle the rigors of a long-term academic assignment, the university is tempted to lower its expectations. This in turn produces a group of young adults even less inclined to make long-term commitments or plans, thereby accelerating the cycle of short-term efforts and achievements.

A second trend might be termed a crisis of confidence and competence. Significant numbers of parents do not feel that they are doing as good a job as they would like to. This sense of inadequacy is not limited to any one socioeconomic, ethnic, or religious group. Struggling with ever-accelerating demands on their time and energy, and by the very real crises which their children are threatened with, parents feel they have failed—a sentiment which does not escape the notice of their children. Students arrive at the university with little or no experience with confident role modeling, anticipating waffling, lack of consistency, or arbitrary decisions from authority figures. While they may unconsciously long for such leadership, students often do not know how to respond to it when they finally encounter it. The university cannot play the part of the parent that it did for so many centuries, yet many of its students seem to need just that.

The relationship between the university and the family has not

---

Row, 1985), 87 ff.

always been as simple and straightforward as some might want to believe. From the founding of European universities in the Middle Ages until the early nineteenth century, young boys barely into their teens entered a strict environment where the university was expected to act *in loco parentis*. Harsh and impersonal regulations of the scholars' lives were interrupted by riotous outbursts of youthful rebellion. While alumni recalled their university days fondly, many of these days were spent in revolt and in rejection of the value system imposed on them. This "patriarchal" era of university life was gradually replaced with a system of academic electives, extracurricular activities, and ever-increasing personal freedom, paralleled by a predictable revolution of rising expectations. The student at a contemporary American Catholic university or college enjoys a range of personal choices unimaginable a century ago. The widening of the student's horizon of options has been regarded as an unalloyed good, as these choices promote responsibility and personal autonomy. Yet while the structure and expectations of the university have been evolving, the preparatory experience of the student has changed. The expectation that universities would function *in loco parentis* decreased, while the pre-collegiate experiences of students lasted longer and were less similar.

It is no longer possible to speak of the university acting *in loco parentis* as the university can no longer make assumptions about the value systems in which its students have been raised. Herein lies the first challenge to American Catholic higher education in the late twentieth century: to provide a cohesive experience to students coming from varied backgrounds.

QUALITY

Inextricably linked with questions about "consumers" and "products" of higher education is the issue of the quality of the students and faculty who choose to work at a particular institution. Quality is a difficult concept to define in a few words: it is also a notion that evolves over time. The medieval masters of the University of Paris and the founders of colonial Harvard College had demonstrably different notions of what constituted a quality student or instructor than most of us would hold today. Society in bygone eras expected different skills, attitudes, and religious commitments from members of its university communities. Until just the other day, relative to the history of higher education, at least outward conformity to an established religious doctrine was a key determinant in the acceptance of teacher or student within most universities and colleges.

Except for a small (but not yet negligible) minority of institutions, the days of religious commitment forming the most important criterion for admission are over for good. Instead, those schools lucky enough to be selective in their choice of faculty and student body rely on demonstrations of ability to make their decisions. For students, this may mean grades and test scores; for selection of faculty, teaching evaluations and publication records are most important. Controversy has swirled around both the procedures of standardized testing and faculty hiring practices for some time. In both cases, much of the debate centers on whether these procedures are "fair," i.e., whether they, in fact, identify the most able candidates *and* provide a range of candidates reflective of our country's diversity. While much remains unresolved in each of these debates, we will pass over the issues of fairness and accuracy to consider the problem specifically from the point of view of the American Catholic university.

First, students. Students, like all human beings, come in varying levels of native ability, motivation, physical and mental health, pre-collegiate academic preparation, and socio-economic status. Assuming that a standardized test such as the SAT or ACT could be made entirely free of cultural bias—and that is assuming a good deal—the performance of prospective college freshmen on such a test should reflect all of the above variables except perhaps the last one. Test scores would then suggest a wide range of degrees of readiness for college among students, which is, in fact, what the test designers claim is the case. Now the process of sorting begins, with the students earning the highest test scores and high school grades seeking admission, hopefully, to some of the "best schools," while others with less stellar scores set their sights on state institutions with broader admissions policies, and so on. To use the language of marketing, a diverse group of consumers chooses from among thousands of service providers to find the provider that will meet each of their needs, while the providers each seek to establish market niches.

We must be cautious in using the market analogy, however, because there is a constant upward shift in the establishment of many academic market niches. J. C. Penney's does not claim the same clientele as Saks Fifth Avenue, but many universities seek constantly to upgrade their academic reputations through comparisons with more prestigious institutions. One way to become known as one of the "best schools" is to raise admission standards, a move that is generally popular with all concerned (except those denied admission). But what does such a move mean for a Catholic university? There are several answers to this question, the most important one being that by raising standards a Catholic institution appears to be reversing a trend that has gone on for most of the century; that is, the undervaluing of these institutions relative to other colleges and universities in America. William P. Leahy has pointed out that in the past, by focusing on teaching and pastoral concerns, ". . . . only a few Catholic higher educational institutions exceeded the general improvement in American higher education and advanced significantly in academic reputation."[3]

By raising admission standards Catholic higher education institutions can gain the prestige and prominence in the wider world that helps assure, among other things, that more students with high test scores will want to apply. But there is a great danger in Catholic institutions of higher learning embracing the value system of the majority of prestigious American universities if the costs and the risks of such a move are not examined first. Any institution, Catholic or not, that decides to make its admissions policies stricter must ask: who will benefit? In general, faculty are in support of higher admissions standards, as this will mean more capable students in the classroom. Administrators tend to approve as well, since higher standards add luster to their institutions. Yet not every university is able nor wishes to join the Ivy League, and there is almost always a limit to how much more restrictive admission can become. In the meantime, if effort is diverted away from the two activities that Leahy has identified as traditional concerns of Catholic higher education, teaching and pastoral concerns, something important may be lost, and the Catholicity of the institution may well be, in many people's view, in jeopardy. An equally important concern stems from the urban and frequently impoverished environments in which the majority of American Catholic universities

---

[3] William P. Leahy, S.J., *Adapting to America: Catholic Jesuit and Higher Education in the Twentieth Century* (Washington, DC: Georgetown UP, 1991), p. 146. Considering the leadership positions which Catholic universities have occupied through much of history, this is a serious charge.

are located. The quest for "quality" students may deny opportunities to the very individuals living in the shadow of the University who could benefit most.

Although some have framed the debate as a question of Catholic identity on the one hand versus academic excellence on the other, we believe that it is not necessary to view the debate as a zero-sum game. Quality students are not necessarily born, they grow, and the growth can be furthered. When a university coordinates its curriculum with selected secondary schools from which it typically recruits, several benefits can result. Not only will the university be more assured of the training of its incoming freshmen, but the secondary school can provide a more academically focused program for its college-bound students.

Another conclusion that flows from the current status of family life in this country is that while espousing the highest ideals in their mission statements, Catholic colleges and universities must be realistically modest and honest about their success in achieving the excellent goals, both moral and intellectual, of their mission. Rather than pointing the finger to the deteriorating quality of family life and early defective childhood education of their students, Catholic institutions should be in the forefront of challenging their faculties, staff, and resources to reach out and down into the early life and education of their future students. Admittedly this is a pioneering, relatively unexplored, and potentially dangerous field, but here again, a Jesuit university should be eager to accept the challenge. While the success of efforts such as community-based programs, Family Center, and other outreach cooperative childhood and youth programs on the part of our School of Social Service and other University personnel cannot be definitely assessed until a future date, yet we are enthusiastic that the University is accepting these difficult new facets of a Catholic university's responsibility and accountability in directing faculty efforts toward the goal of service.

Which brings us to the question of faculty excellence. As we have noted earlier, excellence in scholarship or research appears to be easier to ascertain in the short run than excellence in teaching. Overlapping with and influencing an instructor's ability to conduct successful research is his or skill at obtaining grant money. The modern university who recruits a successful grant writer not only stands to benefit from the fruit of funded research, but also gains an important source of potential income as well as a reputation as a university which wins grants. But along with the principle of "market value," which decrees that a business professor must be paid more than a philosophy professor because of the greater demand for the former in the outside world, comes the reality that different academic disciplines likewise have varying potentials for obtaining research funding. Again, the sciences and the professions typically offer more opportunities for large-scale outside funding than the humanities.

All these elements unfortunately blur the perception of what constitutes faculty excellence. How can the "quality" of an effective grant winner be weighed against the accomplishments of an outstanding teacher, or against those of a researcher working in a field where there is relatively little grant money available? Will attracting a scientific or scholarly superstar to an academic department promote more excellence among his or her peers, or will it only fuel jealousy and resentment?

It may seem to be unwarranted boldness to claim to have answers to all these questions but we maintain that there are ways to reduce the severity of the problems mentioned here. Let us first consider the often remarked upon values conflict between rewarding the researcher/grant recipient and rewarding the outstanding teacher or mentor. There is no easy one-step solution to this dilemma, but there are ways to level the playing field—if indeed the issue must be seen as a competition. First, the university must recognize that the successful researcher or grant recipient has tangible evidence of achievement, and that the superior teacher needs the same means of identifying his or her accomplishment. Let all academic departments in a university identify their outstanding teachers through awards, grants, or some other public means. The process must not stop here but needs to be sustained institutionally throughout the academic year. The various aspects of effective teaching—communication skills, use of information technologies, mentoring, faculty/student collaboration, and others—have already been the topics of symposia, workshops, and presentations at Saint Louis University. These measures not only communicate information and ideas about the act of teaching, but they also raise the visibility of this act amid the competing agendas of the university.

All of the above, however, can turn out to be mere window dressing if growth and excellence in teaching is not embedded in the institutional policy for tenure and promotion. In recent years the publication requirements for tenure and promotion have tended to rise at many American universities and colleges. This is not a damaging trend, since research places the instructor in touch with the cutting edge of the discipline and may compel him or her to rethink the discipline in ways that will enhance its presentation to students. However, increased accomplishments in research are by themselves insufficient grounds for promotion or tenure in any institution that alleges to value teaching. There are two ways out: unambiguous documented growth of supposedly equal dimensions in both teaching or research, or the creation of two distinct tracks to professional advancement, one stressing teaching and the other research. We propose the latter course. No instructor would be allowed to neglect one area, but each candidate would appeal for advancement based on a self-identified emphasis in one or the other field. Research standards would not need major revision, while evaluation of teaching could be based at least initially on an accepted model such as Schulman's proposal for assessment of teaching.[4] Such an approach could be modified to address the special characteristics of teaching in different departments or programs. We admit that the initial results of such a program may not satisfy everyone, but the university's continued trumpeting of its high esteem for teaching in the face of evidence to the contrary is surely worse.

Finally, universities must confront professional jealousy, the perennial occupational disease of academics. No program can eradicate this destructive emotion, but providing more than one avenue for professional recognition and advancement can lessen the sting of resentment. We must also strive, through modeling from administrators and through demonstrated institutional commitments, to exalt the concept of service among faculty, and to discourage self-focused, atomizing careerism. Any university, Catholic or otherwise, which can successfully place the ideal of service squarely at the top of the agenda of all faculty will have done much to preserve worthwhile institutional values.

---

[4] Lee Schulman, "Assessment for teaching: An initiative for the profession," *Phi Delta Kappan* 69:38–44.

CONCLUSION

LOVE IS UNION UNDER THE CONDITION OF PRESERVING ONE'S
INTEGRITY.

—ERICH FROMM, THE ART OF LOVING

No other society on earth offers such a diverse range of post-secondary educational options as does the United States. It follows that a wide range of definitions of excellence exists among our colleges and universities. At the same time there are powerful mainstream trends in higher education that include emphasis on product rather than process and a consumerist attitude among students. A university can dare to ignore or downgrade these trends only if it is clear about its own values and its ability to attract students and teachers who share these values. The American Catholic university of the next century cannot turn to examples from its own history for definitive solutions to this problem; rather it must continue to invent itself, steering a course between rigid rejection of the surrounding society and placid acquiescence to every trend or fad. This middle course is the most difficult of all, for not only is it as yet uncharted, but it is sure to be less than acceptable to those holding extreme positions on either side. As the university responds to changing circumstances it needs an anchor, a point of reference from which to assess each new challenge. No better point of reference for the American Catholic university can be found than love, in the simultaneously broad and elevated sense of the Greek *agape* about which Jacques Maritain has written:

> What does a great deal for virtue is love, because the basic hindrance to moral life is egoism, and the chief yearning of moral life is liberation from oneself, and only love, being the gift of oneself, is able to remove this hindrance and bring this yearning to fulfillment. . . . Love, human love as well as divine love, is not a matter of training or learning, for it is a gift . . . that is why it can be the first precept. How could we be commanded to put into action a power which we have not received or may not first receive? There are no human methods or techniques of getting or developing charity, any more than any other kind of love. There is nevertheless

education in the matter: an education which is provided by trial and suffering, as well as by the human help and instruction of those whose moral authority is recognized by our conscience.[5]

Because love is not culturally derived and is not learned, it is also immutable, non-negotiable, and ultimately indestructible; it is the basis from which inquiry, dialogue, and growth begins. Only if the members of the university community approach the decisions they must make and the conflicting forces vying for the attention and support of the university with love rather than defensiveness or a spirit of intolerance will it be possible for the American Catholic university to maintain the middle course with integrity. In practical terms this means affirming the commitment of the university to the message of the Gospels as it is understood in the Catholic tradition while welcoming a diversity of opinion in all areas of university discourse. It means making clear that the university places a unique value on the Catholic and Jesuit expressions of spirituality which it will constantly strive to interpret to a changing world. At the same time dialogue with representatives of other traditions and interpretations will always be welcome, provided that all parties treat one another with respect. If the university is secure in its own sense of identity, there will be no risk to the integrity of the institution, and no danger that its deeds will be compromised or forgotten.

---

[5] Jacques Maritain, *Education at the Crossroads* (New Haven: Yale UP, 1957), p. 95–96.

CHAPTER
TEN
MYSTERY[†]

*THERE IS NOTHING BEAUTIFUL OR SWEET OR GREAT IN LIFE
THAT IS NOT MYSTERIOUS.*

—FRANÇOIS-RENÉ DE CHATEAUBRIAND

The modern American Catholic university, beset by all of the curricular, administrative, and political distractions that occupy its secular counterparts, has an additional and largely unique responsibility. It must do more than merely provide an environment where certain ethical principles are observed and where responsible thinking and conduct are promoted. The Catholic university must continue to be a place where the spiritual dimension of life is affirmed and explored, not as a peripheral or isolated activity, but as the heart and *raison d'être* of the institution. The Catholic university is concerned with challenges not just of this life but the mysteries of the life to come, and the latter are ultimately of more significance than the former. The Catholic university is committed to a dualistic view of humanity in which the visible and physical is complemented by the

---

[†] This chapter has been previously published under the title "The Catholic University's Recognition of Mystery," in *America*, 27 May 1995, p. 17–20, 32–35.

139

invisible and the spiritual. While the content of curriculum, the modes of instruction, and the ways in which the university interacts with its surroundings are negotiable, this commitment to the unseen world of the spirit is not.

This said, we must quickly add that it is not the role of the Catholic university in America to convert the non-Catholics in its midst or to claim that Church teachings have an exclusive monopoly on the truth. The central importance of spirituality on which the Catholic university insists does not require it, or any other educational institution, to proselytize among its students or neighbors. We acknowledge that the Catholic university should promote the ideas expressed in the documents of the Church while simultaneously respecting and affirming other belief systems that also view human beings as possessing a soul as well as a body. Thus the stance of the university regarding the nature of human persons is a broad one in comparison with views held in previous centuries.

Critics may see the above position as the selling out of a formerly more aggressive (or self-defensive) stance that stressed the unique qualities and the divine origins of Church doctrine. But the Catholic university's welcoming of other belief systems does not negate its commitment to teaching, within the context of departments of theology, what the Church has held to be true, nor does it mean that religious questions framed from a Catholic perspective have no place in the Catholic university. David J. O'Brien, Loyola Professor of Roman Catholic Studies at the College of the Holy Cross in Worcester, Massachusetts, has expressed this point well:

> Catholic schools have a special responsibility to attempt to integrate religious questions into general education and to offer interested students, including those in professional and graduate programs, opportunities to engage the Catholic tradition and to learn of the life and work of the contemporary church. They also share with all other schools an obligation to assist faculty and students to think through their social and civic responsibilities, especially in the context

of the specific forms of learning they pursue.[1]

SENSE OF THE SPIRITUAL

Professor O'Brien's acknowledgment that the students involved be "interested" is important, as is his mention of graduate students, for recognition of the unseen and mysterious is as important in a medical school class as it is in an undergraduate theology course. This task of teaching about the mysterious is in one sense more difficult than it was a few decades ago. Trends in mainstream American culture leave many students and more than a few instructors uncomfortable discussing the spiritual, even if privately they acknowledge its existence. The decline in enrollments at parochial or private high schools also means that fewer students enter a place like Saint Louis University with the background to begin relatively sophisticated discussions of religious experience. The formal religious background of graduate and professional students is even more varied and unpredictable than that of undergraduates and is an accurate reflection of the increasing diversity found on Catholic university campuses. Moreover, the typical competition and the psychological and financial pressures of graduate education pose a special challenge to Catholic universities that have few professors trained in theology and that hope to address issues of the spirit as well as of the mind.

These universities must therefore rely on lay teachers, on non-Catholics, and even on the agnostic and atheist to get their message across. The time is long past for bemoaning these developments or for trying to generate formulas to determine the exact number of Catholics, or the spiritually inclined, needed to insure the "Catholicity" of a Catholic university. Even if a "critical mass" of teachers committed to Catholic values could be determined, the actual number is far less important than the thoroughness and fairness with which prospective faculty are recruited and interviewed, and the care with which the faculty is educated as to the mission of the university, which ultimately is concerned with encountering the mystery of human life and destiny.

In years gone by, the spiritual needs of students at Catholic

---

[1] David J. O'Brien, "Conversations on Jesuit (and Catholic?) Higher Education: Jesuit Si, Catholic. . .Not So Sure," *Conversations*, 6 (Fall 1994), p. 11.

universities were addressed by a "spiritual director," the direct ancestor of today's campus ministry staff and/or the vice president for mission. Yet a single individual or office cannot adequately meet the needs of a diverse and diffuse student body. For this reason it is all the more important that as large a portion of the entire university faculty as possible become involved in supporting this facet of the university's mission. Delicate questions arise when that faculty is recruited in part according to criteria reflecting this aspect of the mission, but also in part reflecting scholarly or professional accomplishments.

No matter how firmly the university's administration strives to establish clear criteria for hiring, the decisions of departmental hiring committees are influenced by subjective and personal factors, by pressures to recruit faculty who reflect the diversity of the student body and community, and by the availability of appropriate candidates. As if these complications were not enough, the very nature of the interviewing process often makes it difficult to obtain a balanced picture of the candidate. Candidates understandably supply references that show them in the most favorable light, and Federal laws restrict questioning the candidate regarding many personal topics. While these laws appropriately protect candidates from intrusive and harassing questions, they place the Catholic university in the unenviable position of occasionally having to infer the candidate's actual positions on matters relating to the university's spiritual mission. This approach, of course, is very ineffective.

"LISTEN, I WILL TELL YOU A MYSTERY! WE WILL NOT ALL DIE,
BUT WE WILL ALL BE CHANGED, . . ."

— I COR. 15:51

The original meaning of the Greek *mysterion* implied not so much a puzzle to be solved as an initiation into a realm of experience which was visible only to the initiated. A mystery was a rite, a passage, and a transformation. The university engages mystery in this sense of the word as well as in the sense of mystery as humanly unknowable. Embedded in the acknowledgment of the spiritual side of human existence is the inescapable truth that the spiritual side cannot be entirely comprehended. Within the mystery there are both ambiguities to be clarified and subjective experiences which cannot be fully communicated or explained. There is also the unknown, which Church teaching asserts will be known in the next life.

But the university also can provide mystery as the portal through which the initiate passes into an unseen world. This passage, whether the initiation is conceived of in specifically religious terms, or more generally in a personal spiritual awakening, has historically been one of the most powerful attractions of the university. Unlike universities that flourished in medieval France or Renaissance Italy, American Catholic universities operate in a pluralistic democracy with strong traditions of academic freedom and varying modes of inquiry, both of which can function as powerful forces to promote encounters with the mysteries. We therefore agree with the presidents of fifteen American Catholic universities on ordinances proposed to implement *Ex Corde Ecclesiae*, the 1990 pontifical document on Catholic higher education. They pointed out the atmosphere of conflict and even hostility that these ordinances could produce:

> If implemented, we believe that significant harm would be done. .. . Under these ordinances, a university would be put in an adversarial relationship with the local Bishop, who would be expected to judge the competency, orthodoxy, and probity of life of a professional theologian.[2]

Such an adversarial and judgmental atmosphere is not conducive to encounters with mystery, nor does it encourage faculty or students who fear that their beliefs are not acceptable to the Church to enter into productive dialogue with teachers, colleagues, or peers. Entering into the mystery cannot be forced through conformity and should not be compelled through threat or punishment.

MATERIAL NEEDS AND PRAGMATIC RESPONSES

By placing the encounter with mystery at the center of the university experience, the Catholic university finds itself experiencing other

---

[2] Letter of fifteen Catholic university presidents and chairmen of boards of trustees to Bishop John J. Leibrecht, chairman of a U.S.C.C. Committee on this pontifical document, dated November 29, 1993.

tensions. The world view of the empirical scientist need not be inimical to either meaning of the word mystery, but the procedures of modern science are. The agencies that finance the university's scientific endeavors and the outcomes expected from these endeavors do little to engender respect for the idea of mystery in a learning environment.

Again, professional fields such as business and education arguably have a great need for the perspective that the spiritual provides. Yet the material needs and pragmatic responses of these fields generally tend to overshadow the spiritual and mysterious elements of these undertakings. As we speed from crisis to crisis we are apt to forget the spiritual reality that creates the practical imperative. Another risk inherent in embracing mystery comes from an unexpected quarter. Because the mysterious includes the unknowable that appears to us absolute, we may be inclined to view our understanding of mystery as an immutable absolute as well. In reality our understanding of the mystery, both in the sense of the ineffable and of the initiation to the ineffable, evolves over time.

University educators face different social conditions and human responses to these conditions than their predecessors of 100 or even 30 years ago. Our conception of what we must be prepared to tolerate has broadened. The commitment of the Catholic university to what it calls "family values" remains as strong as ever. Nevertheless, its tolerance of those who are not within a traditional nuclear family compels us to extend our Christian love to them, even as we affirm the scriptural and sacramental basis for the sanctity of marriage. Such a position is easily misunderstood. Yet if, as Theodore Hesburgh, C.S.C., former president of the University of Notre Dame, has often said, the university is where the Church does its thinking, this thinking should include paradoxical and at times seemingly contradictory thoughts about daily life and about mystery.

JESUIT UNIVERSITIES IN PARTICULAR

It is by no means certain that, given this necessity for simultaneous acknowledgment of Catholic spirituality and the practical and changing circumstances of human beings within and outside of the Church, Catholic universities will be sustained. The very fact that the future of Jesuit higher education, for example, has become the subject of so much discussion in recent years is an indication of the uncertainty many in

Jesuit universities feel about the future mission of these schools. In the moment of transition from Jesuit to non-Jesuit (or perhaps more properly, post-Jesuit), the Ignatian ideal need not be lost, however. But to assure that what is retained is more substantial than a fading afterglow, deliberate measures must be taken. At Saint Louis University the Faculty Partnership program attempts to begin this process of sharing the original Ignatian mission with lay faculty, but more needs to be done.

The mission of a Jesuit university is closely related to the notion of mystery. Since the time when St. Ignatius Loyola (1491–1556), founder of the Society of Jesus, and his followers began to establish schools throughout the world, the motivation behind Jesuit education has been more than the furthering of human knowledge. If this statement seems only a truism, let us look deeper to see the dilemma concealed within it.

At the foundation of the Jesuit experience lies the *Spiritual Exercises* of Ignatius, a handbook for a searching and often arduous mystical training that emphasizes both the mystery and the necessity of action in the material world. Without the *Spiritual Exercises* there would be no Saint Louis University; yet—and here is the essence of the dilemma—the university today is supported by a faculty the majority of whom, despite their sympathy with the ideas of the Society of Jesus, have not experienced the mystery inherent in this training. If we insist that an encounter with mystery, as elucidated by Ignatius, is central to the university identity, then we must concede that this identity may already be in jeopardy. If, on the other hand, we allow that those who have not undertaken the *Spiritual Exercises* can sustain the Jesuit mission virtually on their own, are we not denying the unique value of these *Exercises*?

No facile answers present themselves in the face of this dilemma. The most desirable outcome would no doubt be to find more men willing and able to embark on the long journey which results in becoming a Jesuit educator. While the Society is, of course, vitally concerned with finding ways of attracting prospective Jesuits, all observers agree that for at least the foreseeable future, the numbers of Jesuits teaching in universities and colleges will continue to dwindle. Other approaches must therefore be considered.

The history of the Society furnishes examples of lay men and women, as well as religious of other congregations, supporting Jesuits in their work, but in these instances the lay workers did not share either the educational responsibilities or institutional authority of members of the Society. In earlier centuries, and even at the beginning of this century, lay partners of Jesuits, who were organized into societies called Sodalities, neither expected nor received recognition as equals. Today the building of partnerships between Jesuit educational institutions and lay men and women teaching in them must be based on a different understanding or partnership. A basic component of this new relationship will be a true equality between Jesuit and partner.

PARTNERS AS EQUALS

During the last half-dozen years the Society of Jesus has begun the process of including lay men and women in its mission. Jesuit Provinces in places as diverse as Ireland, East Asia, and Maryland expressed a desire to develop more aesthetic Jesuit–lay collaboration and to strengthen the collaboration already in existence. Closer to home, the U.S. Jesuits' Wisconsin Province has embarked on a program which seeks to do just this. Entitled Ignatian Associates, the program includes a two-year process culminating in "first promises," public declaration of commitment to the Jesuit mission.

The two-year formation process includes discussions regarding the mission of the Society, study of key Jesuit documents, including the *Spiritual Exercises*, ten to twelve hours per month of service to others, and formation in prayer. The language of the formula for first promises closely parallels the formula for a Jesuit's first vows upon entrance into the Society. The formation and role of Associate should not be seen, however, as merely a watered-down version of a full-fledged Jesuit experience. The broadening of the Jesuit community through the admission of Associates is certainly within the Ignatian tradition of adaptability to varying social circumstances—in this instance, the affiliation of significant numbers of individuals who are willing and able to serve the Ignatian mission.

The Wisconsin Ignatian Associates, who at this writing number less than a dozen, are missioned to diverse individual apostolic commitments ranging from ministry with HIV/AIDS patients to family recreation programs and the teaching of catechism. The Associates program, however, does not yet focus on the specific needs of a Jesuit college or university. Since Major Superiors in the Society are urging experimentation with innovative efforts to create Jesuit-lay partnerships, we would hope that Saint Louis University would be one of the first to design and implement such a critically needed program. Should programs such as the Ignatian Associates be instituted within the framework of higher education, some of the features of the culture of American academe must be considered. The literature on U.S. Catholic higher education is extensive, and we do not pretend that the following list is exhaustive, but we offer it as a starting point for serious discussion about the relationship of an expanded and redefined Jesuit presence.

1. The culture of the contemporary American Catholic university reflects the dynamic evolution of higher education in this country during the past 150 years. Viewed from the point of view of the instructor, the American university system has placed great emphasis upon individual initiative, competition of its scholars, and on contributions to knowledge through a ritual of challenges to existing assumptions. Each of these characteristics holds the seeds of potential conflict with the ideals of obedience that were originally a crucial component of the organization of the Society of Jesus.

    American academics are increasingly socialized to work frequently in isolated competition. Is such an attitude compatible with lay affiliation with a Society that historically has valued solidarity and obedience? The self-selection of voluntarily associated lay persons within a university faculty produces a group of Associates who hold values separate from those held by the majority of the unaffiliated faculty. This separation may weaken rather than strengthen the university as a whole.

2. The dichotomy between the scholarly research activities of faculty members and their other, more interpersonal roles is well-known. In the larger world of American higher education, the former is typically more highly valued than the latter. However, the commitment articulated by Ignatian Associates of the Wisconsin Province can be more easily assessed within the realm of the interpersonal than in the context of pure scholarship. To put it another way, an instructor whose assignment is essentially teaching and counseling students can be guided and mentored by other faculty and by administrators so that he or she can fulfill the promise offered upon becoming an Associate. For a faculty

member whose principal assignment is research or scholarship, assistance from peers may be more difficult and success more elusive. In short, he or she may not get his work published. In an environment where failure to publish results in denial of tenure, such a dilemma could warp the intent of those who promise their fidelity to the Society.

3.　One response to this problem is to allow only tenured faculty or only faculty with primarily teaching assignments to make such promises to the Society, but such a policy would clearly deprive the Society of some of its most motivated potential Associates. Rather, the advent of a program similar to that found in the Wisconsin Province on a university campus should prompt a re-examination of the priorities of the institution and even the criteria for tenure operating in that university. Taking such a step may be risky, but in the long run may prove salutary for the university that possesses only limited resources and can excel only in a few chosen fields.

4.　A university is staffed not only by faculty and administrators, but by coaches, counselors, residence hall directors, and many others. While the support by each of these for the ideals of Ignatius is important to the university, the involvement of residence life staff in the mission of the university is arguably one of the most crucial. The social development of undergraduates is an area where the Jesuit college or university can legitimately claim to be offering an alternative to other schools, and where the notion of a role model can be transformed from rhetoric to reality. We therefore recommend that every effort be made to recruit residence life staff into programs involving special commitment to the mission of the Society.

5.　Graduate students and professional school students make up another part of the university meriting inclusion in any program to expand the range of individuals who can serve the Ignatian mission. The needs and interests of graduate and professional school students, who often have lives based far from the university campus, are too often overlooked by administrators already responding to undergraduates, faculty, and alumni.

Yet, graduate students hold special promise as prospective lay associates. By their choice of graduate education, they have already demonstrated a willingness to make a commitment of time and effort stretching over a period of years. With their demonstration of success in advanced studies, these students confirm their ability to organize their lives around an articulated goal. The curricula of graduate and professional programs are in many cases excellent "fits" for future Associates. Medical ethics, education, public policy, and medicine are among the graduate programs currently offered at Jesuit universities that should be included in the development of lay partnerships.

6.   All Jesuit institutions have faculty, students, and administration who are fully committed to supporting the institution but who are not themselves Catholic. Can such individuals become involved in committed lay partnerships with the Society of Jesus? A century ago such a question would have been unthinkable, but with the growth of an ecumenical spirit we must in all seriousness ask whether the Society can afford to pass over such important potential partners. We must also raise the more difficult issue of the inclusion of non-Christians among those promising to work for the mission of the Society. The broader the range of acceptable candidates becomes, the more inclusive (and, of course, the less specifically Catholic) the wording of their promises will be. Nevertheless, the *Spiritual Exercises*, which have been recognized by no less an authority than Peter-Hans Kolvenbach, Superior General of the Society of Jesus, as beneficial to non-Catholics, can remain the focal point of the process leading up to the offering of promises.[3]

A BROADER COMMUNITY

Earlier we have written about the importance of interpreting the Jesuit university to its surrounding community. The inclusion of lay persons in the educating mission of the Society in new and profound ways also requires careful interpretation to various constituencies. The

---

[3] Letter of September 27, 1991, to Friends and Colleagues of the Society of Jesus.

relationship between the Society of Jesus and a university as a community of teachers with its own chains of command and responsibility, its organization by specialization, and its ties to other institutions will have to be interpreted in light of the promises made to the Society. Jesuits may find that they need to learn more about the procedures of academe, while academics who have made promises will need to consider their professional responsibilities in light of their promises. Everyone in the university community, especially the professional colleagues of faculty Associates, must be educated about the type of commitment they are entering into and what its impact will be on the workings of the university. Moreover, the intentions of the Society in inviting the inclusion of lay persons in its mission need to be discussed openly and candidly. Otherwise, some within the community may conclude that the Jesuits are merely trying cynically to hold onto their control of universities, a point of view that can only promote an antagonistic atmosphere harmful to both the Ignatian mission and the functioning of the university.

There are other constituencies from whom few if any candidates for lay partnership with the university are likely to come, but who deserve a complete and comprehensive interpretation of the role of lay Associates. These include undergraduates, the board of trustees, donors (past and potential), alumni (some recruitment efforts in this direction may be appropriate), government agencies having dealings with the university, and the general public. The level and type of knowledge about the Society possessed by each of these constituencies will determine how the notion of lay partnership is presented. In fact, no aspect of the creation of such a program is more important than the impression of the program held by various groups touched by the university. The long-term success of lay partnerships within a Jesuit university may depend on how well students and community members grasp the significance of the promises made.

Finally, if a reorganization of the American Jesuit provinces along functional rather than regional lines is to be adopted, the integration of lay partnerships will be more easily accomplished. A Province consisting entirely of professed members and lay partners will be better equipped to address the problems of integration, recruitment, and interpretation that we have briefly sketched. Faculty who undertake promises to the Society will feel greater support for their efforts within an organization structured around the concerns of higher education.

And their colleagues are less likely to worry that the goals of higher education are being undermined by an unfamiliar theological agenda if they know that the Society has established an administrative unit exclusively for higher education.

The literature dealing with American higher education has been filled for the past decade with charges that the moral core of the university experience has been compromised or even killed. The development of Jesuit/lay partnerships is not a panacea for the real or imagined ills of the American Catholic university, but it is a way for Jesuit institutions to take the lead on a number of moral fronts. First and foremost will be the promotion within the university tradition of these partnerships that exist in opposition to cynical careerism, excessive competition, and intellectual fragmentation. Even a tiny minority of lay partners, provided they have unimpeachable academic credibility, can contribute greatly to the moral climate of the university. Second, the important component of service to the community will be enhanced and emphasized by the presence of faculty and others committed to an ideal which includes service.

It is encouraging and gratifying to realize that the recent General Congregation 34 of the Society of Jesus gave such a hearty endorsement to the Jesuit/lay cooperation concepts discussed above. Many possible approaches were discussed by the delegates to the Congregation, and Jesuits everywhere were urged to explore multiple ways to achieve more stable and intimate collaboration. For example, it was recommended that there be a ten-year experimentation of "juridical bonding" of individual lay persons to the Society of Jesus. Father General is responsible for evaluating these experiments in various forms of contractual agreements, so that in the not too distant future such contractual agreements may be officially approved.[4] It is entirely possible, therefore, that Jesuit universities will one day count among their members individuals who have publicly promised themselves to God and to service to others, a major breakthrough in Catholic higher education that can be a model for other colleges and universities, Catholic and non-Catholic alike.

We will return now, however, to the central theme of this book, which is the American Catholic university.

---

[4] *GC 34*, D 13, n. 357.

CHAPTER
ELEVEN

THE CHANGING
AMERICAN CATHOLIC
UNIVERSITY

HE WHO ENTERS THE UNIVERSITY WALKS ON HALLOWED GROUND.

—JAMES BRYANT CONANT

In the late twentieth century the remark that the Catholic Church is at a crossroads is a commonplace. American Catholics are aware, albeit in varying degrees, that their Church and the schools it supports are changing rapidly, and that this process of change will continue quite possibly at an accelerating rate. While it lies outside the scope of this book to analyze all the forces that have the potential to redefine what makes up the Catholic educational experience in its totality, some observations about these trends are not out of order.

One of the most visible trends on all Catholic campuses in recent decades has been the steep decline in the numbers of priests and other religious involved in all facets of educational life. This decline echoes a worldwide shortage of clergy and religious that is not limited to the Catholic Church, but which poses special problems for Catholic colleges

153

and universities. For Jesuit universities the problem is more complicated than simply the shrinking of one kind of teaching or research faculty, or even the question of whether the institution can survive without Jesuits at the helm. Ironically, at a point when the actual presence of Jesuits has sunk on some campuses to almost the invisible level, the survival prospects for many Jesuit institutions have never looked better. Saint Louis University is an outstanding example of these two trends. In the early decades of the century, when the University was indisputably the preserve of the Society of Jesus, it functioned almost on a hand-to-mouth basis, with a tiny endowment, severely limited community support, and little national visibility. Today, with an endowment in the hundreds of millions of dollars, a designation by the Carnegie Foundation that places it among the top few dozen research institutions in the nation, and a solid national reputation for teaching, the University is, by any external measure, successful. But is it still in any meaningful way a "Jesuit" institution, when many students spend four or more years without having a Jesuit professor or mentor? On a deeper level, is the designation of Jesuit and even "Catholic" worth fighting over or about? If Saint Louis University and its sister Catholic schools founded by the Jesuits are to retain their designations into the next century, their effectiveness will have to be judged from different criteria than have been used in the past. It is not too far-fetched to imagine a Saint Louis University of the twentieth century with only a few Jesuits on the Board of Trustees, a decreasing number of Jesuits on the faculty, and a student body that is only one-third Catholic, of whom only a small percentage are graduates of parochial schools. Is this a change we can accept? Do we have the capacity to influence such transformation? The entire university community should be involved in a conversation on these topics.

There are various responses to these trends away from the traditionally constituted Catholic university; interestingly, all of these trends take as a given the continuation of the decline in actual presence of the Jesuits at Jesuit universities. Some, such as Holy Cross College's David J. O'Brien, have raised the question whether Catholic universities need to establish some kind of minimum number of Catholics on their faculties in order to provide a "critical mass" of Catholic perspective. Others have asserted that the Catholic or even the Jesuit mission of a school can be maintained by non-Catholic or even non-Christian instructors who are committed to the investigation of the same problems which were the concern of Ignatius and other Catholic teachers. Meanwhile, alumni and parents, educated not so many years ago in a world where "Catholic" appeared to mean something distinct and identifiable, are confused by what seems to be a loss of both a spiritual and cultural point of reference. The past seems lost forever, the future ambiguous and threatening.

While acknowledging these trends which suggest a dilution of the traditional characteristics of Catholic education, we need to keep in mind that many indicators of Catholicism as a world-wide phenomenon do not suggest a decline or dilution. Today, more human beings are counted as members of the Church than at any other time in its two thousand-year history. The patterns of this dynamic growth remind us of the original meaning of "catholic," that is, "kath'olikos," or "through the whole." The Church not only continues to be a world Church, but its make-up increasingly reflects the explosive growth of the developing world, of the number of the world's poor, and of non-Europeans. This world Church is increasingly a community of not only prosperous urbanized heirs of the Greco-Roman civilizations, but also of shanty towns and bare feet. The multiplying, and in many cases diversifying, of the Catholic experience has revealed tensions among groups within the Church who have different understandings of the role of education, and of the university. American Catholic educators, in the Land O'Lakes Statement and elsewhere, have argued for the tolerant and service-oriented role of the American Catholic university within a pluralistic democracy, while the Vatican has occasionally attempted to rein in the more outspoken tendencies of Catholic university instructors. In Latin America, in particular, Catholic university teachers have been among those calling for political justice and social reform, while theology professors in the United States and Europe have sometimes been censured for their open disagreement with traditional teachings of the Church.

This changing and sometimes conflicting character of the world Church and the world itself must be reflected in the reality of a Jesuit university, even one whose traditional mission has been to educate members of its local community. Differing points of view, including those in opposition to Church teaching, deserve to be heard. Only when these opinions convey messages of hate or incite violence should the university exercise its right to censorship. In taking such a position we must acknowledge that not all Catholics agree with such a wide definition of toleration and academic freedom. Pope John Paul II himself, in his Apostolic Exhortation on Catholic higher education, *Ex Corde Ecclesiae*, has given bishops the power to take away the title of "Catholic" from any institution which teaches theology considered to be contradictory to the Church's teachings. While some observers conclude that American bishops will simply ignore this order, the issue remains fundamentally unresolved. The question of the boundaries of academic freedom within which a Jesuit university can and should function is further complicated by the overlapping of the categories of human knowledge. The former has been recognized as the appropriate province of scholars and scientists who work in the university; the latter has been claimed by the Church. But research is frequently driven by moral urgency, and its "objective" findings are often difficult to separate from the moral consequences of the knowledge gained. Where does research on *in vitro* fertilization, homosexuality, or differences in brain functions between males and females cross the line from the pursuit of knowledge into the reframing of questions which are fundamentally moral? How far can the study of the Church itself, its founding documents and dogma, be carried without violating some aspect of the role of the Catholic university?

Not only scientific advances but theoretical and interpretive work by researchers and scholars also test the elasticity and tolerance of the Catholic university as it strives to play several roles: that of transmitter of culture and midwife to innovation. Traditionalists point out that the church is not a democracy; this is historically true, but it is also true that the teachings of the Church have undergone constant organic growth since their inception. The circumstances of the sixteenth century precipitated the Council of Trent, which addressed many questions from a different perspective than had Innocent III in the thirteenth century or Gregory the Great in the eighth century. Unlike the *Magisterium*, the research and teaching agendas of the Catholic university at the end of the twentieth century do not include the task of defining morals. The same productive tension between tradition and changing circumstances will undoubtedly be evident in the coming century and beyond.

Nevertheless, an admission that we must be flexible is not a capitulation to relativism. Paralleling and indeed intertwined with the Catholic university's commitment to free inquiry with all its attendant challenges and hazards are some of the university's oldest non-negotiable responsibilities, one of the most important of which is to provide role models. The changes in the nature of society and in our understanding of ourselves which have occurred in the past one hundred years, and to which universities themselves have contributed in no small degree, make the university's role in standing for a particular set of values more crucial than ever before. The proliferation of choices confronting the individual, the implosion of the family, and the toppling of popular idols are only the most conspicuous developments that have left us without concrete human examples of how to live. Less obvious but equally significant in bringing about this need has been the inability of precollegiate education to offer a coherent moral and intellectual formation to students. The task thus falls to the university to provide this leadership.

While the university performs important functions as a forum for ideas, a setting for research, and a school of professional training, the formation of personality ought to be its most important job. During the past half century of growth and transformation at Saint Louis University, no event has been more striking than the encounters between young men and women and their mentors who appeared in a variety of roles: teacher, priest, coach, or merely friend. These individuals, sometimes by explanation, but more often and more effectively by example, modeled honest and humble confrontation with the dilemmas of life in ways that students never forgot.

Calling the university a molder of character is neither original nor controversial. Yet although few would categorically challenge the call for universities of all stripes to focus attention on the development of the character of the young (and in the era of the "nontraditional student," the not-so-young as well), powerful forces militate against universities giving role modeling and moral development high priority. The formation of character can be established as a goal of university fund-raising activities only indirectly, unlike grant writing, athletic win/loss records, or some kinds of research. Character development resists quantitative interpretation. The positive results of mentoring relationships may not be noticeable for years even to the recipient. Nor are the beneficiaries always able to articulate what it is they have gained. In short, there are no good reasons for focusing the energies of the university on providing role models, except one: there is a crying need for such role models and the university is uniquely equipped to provide such an experience.

We cannot predict with certainty whether any university, Jesuit or not, will live up to the challenge of providing role models to students. We can, however, pose questions that each university contemplating making formation of character and personality one of its primary goals must confront. First, does the institution have a clear enough vision of which traits it wishes to promote? These traits must be more than a hopeful but naïve desire to do good; they must be joined to an intellect, and trained to apply a critical framework to new knowledge acquired.

Does the institution have a means by which instructors and others who function successfully as role models are recruited, retained, and appropriately rewarded without compromising the other missions of the university? Are these role models in place in professional and graduate programs, as well as in undergraduate programs, which have traditionally been regarded as their natural home? Is the institution vigilant in guarding against the potential abuses that can occur in a setting where some are set up as role models for others? Are there opportunities for faculty to serve as role models and mentors to one another, thereby establishing a climate in which faculty move most easily into the role of mentor and model to students? Are there safeguards to prevent these ideals from becoming empty Commencement Day rhetoric? And especially in its mission as a Catholic university, is such a university free and committed to propose as a role model for excellence the human person of Jesus Christ whose values and motivations are clearly documented in the historically valid pages of the New Testament?

The answers to these questions will not be found automatically merely by making the university in question financially solvent, by making admissions standards more competitive, by adding to academic resources, by hiring world famous professors, or even by launching into programs of social service which are compatible with the ideals we have already mentioned. A university can be intellectually excellent and yet lack a soul, and a university even can have an explicitly and eloquently stated mission, yet show little evidence of living up to it. The decisive factor, we would argue, is the human leadership of the university.

Having been assured repeatedly that the Catholic Church belongs to the People of God, not merely to its hierarchy, we must now take special care to explain our position regarding the leadership of a Catholic university. First, we acknowledge that the era of the dictatorial, if visionary American university president, of Columbia's Nicholas Murray Butler, Princeton's Woodrow Wilson, and Chicago's Robert

Maynard Hutchins is over, and rightly so. American universities must inevitably reflect the democratic ideals of the complementary society in which they are situated and whose needs they serve. Nevertheless, balancing the natural tendency of modern American universities to be places of toleration, compromise, and democratic process is the need, in our view, for leadership with both the authority and the capability to make difficult decisions. To some degree this need for leadership is evident in most human organizations; the need is especially great in the modern American university because so many forces are at work to prevent the fulfillment of spiritually derived ideals in the complex academic/research/social development/service enterprise which is the university.

Let us put it another way: a corporation is in the business of selling toothbrushes. This is, one could say, its mission. If its leadership fails to do so (and is found out!) he or she will be removed from power, since there is unanimous agreement among the stockholders and unanimous expectation among consumers as to the business of the corporation. The position of the chief executive officer of a university, and especially a Catholic university, is more complicated. There are far more constituencies demanding attention, not all of which have the spiritual, intellectual, and social goals of the university uppermost in their minds. The university administrator must hear them all (although sometimes he or she would rather not) and take them seriously as directives for action if possible, but then return to the tasks of molding character, balancing freedom of expression with respect for human dignity, and propagating the good news of the Gospels, among others, which are part of the special mission of the university. Under these circumstances, how good a "toothbrush" is produced may not be readily apparent to all observers, and it will be the job of the university administrator to help define the nature of the very product which he or she is helping to create.

The conclusion that we offer is, therefore, in one sense simple, even simplistic, on the one hand, but extremely difficult to guarantee. Part of the job of the university is to be on the lookout for individuals capable of carrying out the challenging task of being a shrewd and organizational leader while remaining committed to the ideals that justify the university's very existence. This process must never cease, and should be openly acknowledged as part of the functions of the university. Up to a point the right leader must be trained and recruited, but equal effort must be expected in locating such individuals, for many of the qualities we have alluded to cannot be taught, and are instead innate. Historically, this continuing search for what Jefferson called, in a somewhat different educational context, "the aristocracy of talent and virtue" was compatible with the educational and organizational structure of many religious orders. The history of the Society of Jesus provides useful examples of the promotion of talent into positions of educational leadership (as well as some textbook cases of what not to do), yet today in drastically changed circumstances there is a limit to the immediate usefulness of these historical examples. We turn now to the future of Jesuit education in the United States, with a proposal for how to make the most of the resources available.

Any discussion about the future of Jesuit education in this country must ultimately come to terms with the administrative organization of the Society and the human resources available to it. As the twentieth century draws to a close, the Society in the United States is divided into ten Provinces. These Provinces, which have evolved through the last century and a half, reflect the traditional organization of the Society according to geographical units. In the time of Ignatius and for centuries afterwards, the idea of organizing the Society's activities along geographical lines made sense. Slow and inefficient lines of communication, the intrusions of wars and epidemics, as well as ethnic and regional animosities made it imperative for the Society in its early years to organize itself whenever possible into geographically coterminous units. This era is now past. Instantaneous electronic communications, the ease of travel by airplane or automobile, and the political stability of the United States all make it possible for us to look at the notion of a "Province" in an entirely new light. The necessity of re-evaluating our notion of a Jesuit Province is made all the more urgent by the shortage of manpower that the Society now faces. Although the historical tradition of the Society has been to organize each Province with about one thousand Jesuits, the reality is that many American Provinces now have only five or six hundred Jesuits. The redundancy and inefficiency that this situation has resulted in has prompted some to propose a geographical consolidation of existing Jesuit Provinces. There is, however, a better, if more radical, solution.

The American Provinces of the Society of Jesus can be reorganized, not along geographic lines, but according to their function. One Province could be exclusively for Jesuit institutions of higher education. The benefits of this approach are obvious and important. Entrance to the "information highway" would allow smaller colleges to tap into the library and other resources of larger institutions. Administrators could have more immediate contact with their colleagues regarding developments in financial aid, opportunities for obtaining grants, and trends in enrollment, to name only a few possibilities. Instructors could enrich their teaching through immediate interactive contact with their peers. The potential for collaborative research among instructors at Jesuit schools would be enhanced. Lastly, and by no means of least importance, the closer affiliation of all Jesuit institutions of higher education would promote a sense of shared identity and mission which will be needed in the years ahead as the Catholicity of these institutions is put to the test. Taking the innovative view of Jesuit Province in terms of mission rather than geography can also reduce regional and institutional rivalries which are always fiercest when resources are scarce.

The creation of a Jesuit "Province of American Higher Education" would open the door for the development of a parallel Province devoted to secondary education. Specifically, the identification, training, and promotion of future university leaders could be more focused. The same benefits mentioned with regard to higher education would apply to a Province for Secondary Education. It should also be noted that fund-raising, an important part of the administration of all Jesuit high schools, could be rendered far more efficient if all high schools throughout the country worked together. The grouping of educators and teachers attuned to the same goals is likely to produce a surge of new ideas and approaches to the challenges that all secondary schools face.

Finally, the Society has become increasingly involved in recent years in issues of pastoral care and social justice. The Church has recognized the usefulness of the Society in addressing the needs of its members at a time while diocesan priests are in short supply, and has encouraged many Jesuits to work in parishes and in other non-academic settings. The reorganization of the American Provinces of the Society along functional rather than geographic lines logically suggests the creation of a Province composed of those Jesuits involved in the apostolic mission of their Society. Again, the grouping of Jesuits with similar missions and training makes sense, both from an administrative and from a mission-related standpoint.

Nevertheless, there are objections to this proposal that must be taken seriously. One has to do with the historically holistic nature of the Jesuit vocation. It is a common occurrence for a member of the Society to work for a few years in a higher education or secondary education setting, and then move on to pastoral work. This integrated view of the mission of the Society might be threatened by a restructuring of American Provinces along strictly functional lines. Instead of seeing themselves as Jesuits, members of the Society might come to view themselves as teachers, researchers, or social workers. Another concern that is certain to be raised centers on the relationship of the Provincial to individual Jesuits. The Provincial is expected to provide *cura personalis* or personal care to each member of the Society under his jurisdiction. If the Provincial is geographically distant from many of those under his care, the argument goes, it will be far more difficult , even with the aid of computers and other technology, to provide the personal contact and care which is required. Finally, the reorganization of Provinces along what are in effect professional lines could promote a heightened sense of professional identity among Jesuits which in many cases is antithetical to the values of the Society.

While each of these objections merits a response, none of the problems described is insurmountable. The integrated nature of the Society could be preserved through continuing exchanges of appropriate personnel among the newly constituted Provinces. Inclusion in one Province that is defined largely by advancing technology need not mean exclusion form other Provinces and other assignments. Linking men and their missions across geographic and professional lines will require careful coordination of existing resources and the willingness of all connected with the Jesuit enterprise to set aside traditionally held views of regional autonomy, localized responsibility and academic "turf." We will never again return to a world where missions are isolated from one another as they were even less than a century ago, and if the Society sees itself only in conventional geographical terms, it will be ignoring the web of interconnectedness which already exists in American culture and which is, in fact, one of its most salient characteristics.

The charge that separation and perhaps unintentional stratification of the Society's members and activities will unduly promote professional identities over an identity as a Jesuit is perhaps the most serious criticism which can be made of this proposal. Professional affiliations rather than familial, regional, or religious affiliations have come to define many individuals in our society. Should this tendency, which has already made inroads into the culture of many church-affiliated enterprises, gain a foothold within Jesuit institutions, surely something important would be lost. Yet the very scarcity of isolated Jesuits at Jesuit-run universities, colleges, secondary schools, and other institutions run by the Society may be able to prevent this from happening. A physically isolated Jesuit, linked in a meaningful way with his peers through technology, but working in a school or university, can still retain his identity in the face of pressures to become socialized primarily as an academic or teacher. The physical presence of a community is undoubtedly an important enhancement to anyone's sense of corporate identity, but the history of the Society, from the time of Xavier and Ricci to the present, has shown that it is not essential. As long as Jesuits are inculturated through their lengthy training to see themselves, first and foremost, as members of the Society of Jesus, they can make use of this isolation from other Jesuits in a positive way to reflect on and refocus their sense of identity.

Lurking behind this and all other discussions on the organizational restructuring of the Society in the United States is the shortage of Jesuits. Specifically, the Society of Jesus faces the same decline in the number of candidates for the priesthood that other teaching orders of the Church are confronting. While this phenomenon may be merely a symptom of a collection of less obvious root causes, the result is far from obscure. Jesuit institutions are confronted with the challenge of maintaining their identity and their mission without an assured presence of Jesuit teachers and role models. One response is the increased involvement and commitment, in a systematic and institutionally recognized fashion, from non-Jesuit faculty, as we propose in Chapter X. But it would be ingenuous to ignore the obvious solution of identifying, recruiting, and training more Jesuits to be leaders in higher education. Clearly this is not an easily executed solution, or else we would already be seeing a rise in the numbers of men entering the Society with the intention of serving as educational leaders. Certain questions about the future teaching mission of the Society need to be raised, not merely in the pages of scholarly journals, but in more open forums among all who are concerned about the survival of the Jesuit educational mission. These questions include: What are the known reasons for the worldwide decline in vocations? Are there differences in the pattern of recruitment between the Society of Jesus and other Catholic orders? Are some orders faring better than others? Are there any discernible patterns across the country or the world in recruitment into the Society of Jesus? Are there lessons to be gleaned from the history of the Society that would shed light on the present situation? Who would want to be a Jesuit in the twenty-first century and why?

As all questions intended to provoke serious discussion, the issues raised here are politically hazardous. The answers they may produce, or even the discussions that they could stimulate, may prove embarrassing to some. Or after much hard work we may find that there are no readily apparent answers to these questions—a troubling outcome to be sure. Still, the most probable alternative to a candid exploration of this crisis is the continued diminution of the Jesuit presence in American higher education. Such a development, accepted without a struggle, would be an unworthy concluding chapter for the story of American Jesuit education. Even the most trenchant critics of the Society have always conceded that Jesuits never shied away from seemingly impossible situations. It would be unfortunate if this hard-won reputation were called into question when there remains so much yet to be done.

CHAPTER
TWELVE

SAINT LOUIS
UNIVERSITY: TODAY
AND TOMORROW

TEACH US, GOOD LORD, TO SERVE YOU AS YOU DESERVE:
TO GIVE AND NOT TO COUNT THE COST;
TO FIGHT AND NOT TO HEED THE WOUNDS;
TO TOIL AND NOT TO SEEK FOR REST;
TO LABOR AND NOT ASK FOR ANY REWARD
SAVE THAT OF KNOWING THAT WE DO YOUR WILL.

—SAINT IGNATIUS OF LOYOLA, 1491–1556

SAINT LOUIS UNIVERSITY TODAY

The past fifty years and the changes that they have brought to Saint Louis University are in many ways representative of the general transformation of American higher education which has taken place since the Second World War. It is easy to point to the places where the University has experienced changes common to many other institutions: growth in student body, expansion and reorganization of the curriculum, greater material resources, heightened visibility in the community, and the raising of academic standards. Less

165

obvious but more revealing of the institution itself and its future are those experiences that are unique to Saint Louis University. In retrospect, these events, many of which are chronicled on the preceding pages, can be grouped into three categories. We may call these categories heritage, personalities, and environment. The heritage of the University is, for most of the University community, the least visible but, arguably, the most important of the three. This heritage has both a local and a universal element. The local element is linked to the growth of the city of St. Louis and to the interests of the people who settled in the region. Yet a broader perspective was always present in the goals of the University. From the beginning, when classes at the struggling frontier academy were offered in two languages, French and English, and the student body included young men from Louisiana and Mexico as well as from St. Louis, the University has been concerned with the greater world. These concerns receive support from the other element of the University's heritage.

The Jesuit tradition, established in a now far-off time and place, but possessing the potential for adaptation to other circumstances, remains for the University an inheritance that defines its future. From this inheritance comes the dual objectives of spiritual growth and intellectual development which maintains a productive tension with one another. The growth of the University during the past five decades has produced clear gains in the area of academic excellence. To cite only one statistic, ACT test scores have risen steadily in recent years, with 29% of entering freshmen now scoring above 28. While any standardized test is admittedly an indicator of only limited value, there is much additional evidence to suggest that the University is both attracting and supporting academic talent. The objective of spiritual growth does not, of course, lend itself to quantitative analysis and is always subject to differing interpretations, but the commitment of the University to the sustaining of its spiritual mission is evidenced in a number of ways. These include the creation of a new mission statement, and an increase in the number of Jesuits in teaching positions. The greatest challenge in the spiritual domain, however, is not explained through numbers but instead is found in the complex interplay between the message of the Gospels which the University seeks to spread and the secular world in which the University goes about its business. The outside world affords both the greatest opportunities for the fulfillment of its spiritual mission and paradoxically the greatest risks of being distracted from this goal. How this relationship with the world will be played out depends to a large degree on the personalities of those at the University.

In the light of such a sketchy and necessarily superficial review of the past fifty years I have devoted to Saint Louis University, I would certainly not be so presumptive as to assert that all my varied activities fit neatly into a pattern of pre-conceived priority goals. I do feel, however, that as my years of service unfolded, I was blessed with the awareness that so much of the resources and especially the motivating institutional thrust of Saint Louis University could be fundamentally characterized as "for others," service-oriented, not looking for personal or institutional influence, power, or wealth except insofar as such resources could be used for greater service to society and the greater glory of the God to whom this institution is fundamentally dedicated.

Here might be the appropriate place to express heartfelt gratitude to several individuals and groups whose influence and inspiration helped me maintain a strong spiritual motivation through the long years of preoccupation almost entirely with "worldly" activities—administrative stress, financial strains, fund-raising pressures. About ten years into the Presidency, I became increasingly aware that, of necessity, I was totally walled off from priestly spiritual work. In the 1960s increasing numbers of men and women religious were choosing to make "directed" one-on-one annual retreats instead of "preached" retreats. Fr. John English, S.J., at that time the well-known Director of the Renewal Center in Guelph, Ontario, was scheduled to offer a seminar at the University on the giving of directed retreats, and I signed up. Shortly thereafter some friends of mine among the School Sisters of Notre Dame were kind enough to invite me to be a member of their directed retreat team. Ever since I have been blessed with the apostolic opportunity of participating annually in at least one or two eight-day directed retreats, mostly involving the School Sisters of Notre Dame or the Precious Blood Sisters of O'Fallon. Growing out of this experience came numerous requests to serve as spiritual advisor to various priests, religious women, and a few lay men and women—an exchange from which I have personally profited spiritually far more than those who were seeking direction from me. One thing is sure: the faith and optimism kept alive by these spiritual experiences accounts more than any other single causality for the faith and optimism that I still cherish today.

Also, before concluding this unconventional history of Saint Louis University, it would seem only fair, in spite of the hazards of fallible human memory, to list at least some of the leaders in the past seventy-five years whose foresight and courage have helped to bring the University to its present strong position. I have chosen to note the following:

AMONG THE LAITY:

1.   Gustave Klausner, who with Fr. "Buck" Davis launched the University's first professional business programs.

2.   Dr. Edward Doisy, brilliant biochemist whose winning of the Nobel Prize in 1943 brought visibility and prestige to our Medical Center, and whose generosity in establishing an Endowment Fund (now totaling nearly $100 million) from patent rights income has enhanced the teaching and research performance and provided excellent physical facilities for on-going research in the School of Medicine.

3.   The William McBride Family and descendants, especially Adelaide and Dan Schlafly and Ed and Katherine Walsh.

4.   Mrs. John Janes, the only benefactor of the University, I believe, whose generosity enabled us to establish multiple endowed professorships.

AMONG THE JESUITS:

1.   Frs. Alphonse Schwitalla, James Macelwane, Thurber Smith, William McGucken, Wilfred Mallon, Robert Henle, Jerry Marchetti —each of whom was a pioneering force in expanding the graduate and professional programs, raising academic standards, accentuating research, and introducing sound business practices and accountability.

2.   Fr. Walter Ong, probably the best internationally known scholar, Jesuit or lay, in the University's 175-year history. Even as I write, Walter Ong is about to be honored once again by the Midwest Modern Language Association in a symposium that will have topics with such impressive titles as: 'Ong and the Future of Rhetorical Studies' and 'Venturing into Postmodern Teaching and Scholarship: Walter Ong as Guide and Companion.'

3.   Fr. Maurice McNamee for his life-long dedication to perpetuating study and love of the fine arts, especially through his tireless work to make Cupples House the "jewel" of our Frost Campus.

4.   Fr. Lawrence Biondi: In addition to the unique contributions to the

growth and strengthening of the University on the part of my successors as President who were briefly mentioned on pages 63 and 64, particularly Fr. Edward Drummond, S.J. and Fr. Thomas Fitzgerald, S.J., very special recognition is due Fr. Lawrence Biondi, S.J. In the nine years since his inauguration, Fr. Biondi has developed a dramatic vision of the University as it moves into the twenty-first century. And very substantial elements of that vision have already become reality.

To begin with the most visible and tangible: over $220 million has been expended to achieve an expanded, well-defined, and beautiful Frost (main) Campus, at once urban and contemplative, a source of pride and ownership to students, faculty, and staff alike. A central plaza running east and west for several blocks on both sides of Grand Boulevard ties together the older structures with over $22 million of new and improved buildings and attractive landscaping including restored and renovated buildings—Xavier, DeMattias, McGannon, Wuller, and O'Brien Halls, conversion of Fusz Memorial to the already nationally recognized Museum of Contemporary Religious Art (MOCRA), as well as an excellent student residence hall. At the eastern extremity of this several-block long mall are excellent outdoor athletic fields for baseball, soccer, and field hockey. Throughout this attractive expanse are beautiful fountains, sculptures, and flowered plazas. For the first time in University history, there is adequate parking for faculty, students, and staff, either in garages or surface lots at the campus periphery. The centerpieces of the mall, just west of Grand Boulevard, are the John Connelly Clock Tower and fountains.

By the time this volume appears, major additional improvements will be underway, particularly to enlarge the facilities of our Law School on the west side of Grand on Lindell Boulevard, and buildings on the east side of Grand on Lindell will become the home of Parks College, which will be moving from Cahokia, Illinois, to the Frost Campus in 1997.

Throughout his tenure, Fr. Biondi has frequently emphasized that the attractive campus environment is not an end in itself but rather intended to create an environment conducive to more intensive academic efforts on the part of both faculty and students. And during the last decade there has been ample evidence of significant academic growth and economic vitality. To mention only a few examples: a) the number of endowed professorships to which outstanding scholars have been appointed has risen to approximately 40; b) the Carnegie

Foundation has raised the University to the status of a Research Category II institution, shared by only two other Catholic universities; c) in addition to updated and strengthened academic programs, most schools of the University have added centers for specialized studies, for example, the Jefferson Smurfit Center for Entrepreneurial Studies in the School of Business and Administration, and the Emerson Electric Center for Business Ethics in both the Business School and the College of Arts and Sciences; d) while student enrollment, contrary to the trend in many private universities, has steadily increased, so have the number of brighter students, to the point that ACT scores currently average 25; e) at least partially responsible for brighter students is the ever-increasing availability of endowed scholarship assistance aimed at attracting both highly motivated and academically talented students who are particularly attracted to our Jesuit philosophy of preparing themselves not only for their own future career but also for a life that places a high priority on service "for others"; f) substantial increase in every aspect of diversity, e.g., administrative diversity (about one-half of our administrative personnel are women) and cultural diversity (the Medical campus playing a key role); g) increased financial stability as evidenced by the fact that over the last decade the University's endowment has grown to well over $400 million; and h) the most ambitious fund-raising campaign in University history—$200 million, with a year and a half of the five-year period still remaining—has achieved approximately 86% of the goal—$172 million.

Finally, Fr. Biondi has continued the commitment begun 50 years ago to work cooperatively with the surrounding Midtown community to dedicate its resources and influence to the stabilization and healthy growth, for example, of the Performing Arts district north of us on Grand Boulevard, to help redevelop the ill-fated Laclede Town area east of our campus, and to strengthen and rehabilitate the residential and commercial areas adjacent to the University's Health Sciences Center on S. Grand.

Given this overview of the University and its many constituencies in this the 180th year of its existence, let us confront the future, looking first at major obstacles to continued healthy developments and then to the most all-embracing hopes I cherish for the Saint Louis University of the twenty-first century.

THE FUTURE OF SAINT LOUIS UNIVERSITY

What does the future hold for the Catholic identity of Saint Louis University? There is reason for guarded optimism, although several facts must be met squarely. The first of these is that the number of Jesuits in the United States, both absolutely and relative to the number of Catholics, has been decreasing for some time and will continue to do so. Although the Society of Jesus is still the largest Catholic religious order in the world, its ranks are not only getting thinner, they are also becoming grayer. This numerical decline and aging process echo patterns found throughout the clergy of many denominations in this country, and does not necessarily point to any unique deficiencies within the Society, yet it does threaten the continuation of the mission commenced by St. Ignatius four and a half centuries ago. The response of Saint Louis University and many other Jesuit schools is to try to identify and emphasize what it means to be Catholic in the religious sense as well as catholic in the generic sense. This involves the recruitment of teachers who may not even be Catholic but who are committed to the educational ideals first developed by the Jesuits in the sixteenth century. These men and women also need to share in some way the appreciation for the spiritual motivation that animated the original Jesuits. The special challenge of an institution such as Saint Louis University will be to identify this appreciation among applicants for its teaching positions. Whether this broader definition of the Jesuit educational mission will be sufficient to preserve the Ignatian tradition cannot be said with certainty at this time.

There is a threat to the survival of the Catholic university greater than the presence of faculty hostile or indifferent to the mission of the institution. This is the dilution of the unique Catholic identity of the University to the point that the institution is simply a place where students and faculty are "nice," and where liberal norms are observed more out of a sense of courtesy than conviction. In such a school the ethical consequences of the Christian faith become indistinguishable from the positions held by conscientious and compassionate atheists or agnostics. Having argued for a broad base of tolerance in the university, it may seem strange that we are now appearing to take the position of conservatives, both Catholic and non-Catholic, who are calling for boundaries to tolerance. In reality, the choice is not between more tolerant and accepting and less tolerant and judgmental. It is a choice between the grounds for tolerance. If tolerance, on the university campus or elsewhere, is derived from a recognition of the relatedness of all human beings as children of the same God, there is less chance of lapsing into a comfortable niceness that avoids both conflict and commitment. Tolerance expressed as only the absence of intolerance and based on an ill-defined desire not to offend or rock the boat will not survive the crucibles of the political arena, or the urban streets right outside the university's door. Such a soft tolerance, insubstantial as it is, will not even survive, as it is no match for the harsher world that has intruded into many of the most famous universities. In *Harvard Diary*, Robert Coles wrote, "She began to realize that being clever, brilliant, even what gets called 'well-educated' is not to be equated with being considerate, kind, tactful, even polite or civil." We need positive reasons to resist the temptation to savage our peers in the classroom or the faculty meeting, and an infinitely diluted Catholicity will be as unable to provide those reasons as infinitely diluted Congregationalism has proven for Yale.

Another factor affecting the future of Saint Louis University as a Catholic, Jesuit institution has to do with larger changes in society that leave high school graduates less certain of their own values and identities. In the past it might be argued that the Jesuits did their "best work" in the high schools, where they were able to inculcate attitudes and skills to young men. In the late twentieth century the university has frequently become the place where students seek to develop a meaningful philosophy of life. If Saint Louis University can successfully assume the role of an environment that helps students make good decisions, an important strand of the Ignatian tradition will be preserved.

Saint Louis University has faced difficult times before, as has the city and the community in which it is located. Unlike literally hundreds of colleges and universities founded in this country before the Civil War, the University has not only survived, but has prospered and grown. Given the highlights of the university's growth as well as the many obstacles overcome during the last fifty years, the question now arises: what does Fr. Reinert hope for Saint Louis University as we move into the twenty-first century?

As I attempt to project my chief hopes for the future of the University, let me issue a warning: don't expect any surprises—all five of my most fervent hopes have been discussed in one or more of the preceding chapters. Also, the order in which these hopes are listed is not necessarily an indication of my evaluation of the importance and urgency of each category—all five, in my opinion, must be urgently sought after if Saint Louis University is to reach the level of quality and achievement to which I believe it is called in the years ahead.

HOPE I

As discussed in Chapter X, I would hope that constant, organized effort will develop within the University family—administration, faculty, and staff—a bona fide partnership between dedicated lay men and women and their Jesuit counterparts, thus creating an educational community with acceptance of and commitment to the mission of Saint Louis University in the Ignatian tradition. General Congregation 34 says it best: "Partnership and cooperation with others in ministry is not a pragmatic strategy resulting from diminished manpower; it is an essential dimension of the contemporary Jesuit way of proceeding, rooted in the realization that to prepare our complex and divided world for the coming of the Kingdom requires a plurality of gifts, perspectives and experiences, both international and multi-cultural." [1]

HOPE II

As discussed in Chapter II, I would hope that in every school of the University, there would be required experiences in service learning, emphasizing the combinations and interrelatedness of service praxis and academic learning and reflection. The gauge of our success should be whether our graduates prove to be "men and women for others."

HOPE III

As discussed in Chapter XI, I would hope that each of the 28 Jesuit colleges and universities would be strengthened by much more cooperative academic relationships between administration, faculty, and students. The model of the SLU–Rockhurst college consortium should be expanded. Also the realistic potential of reconstituting the ten American Provinces on the basis of mission rather than geography should be seriously explored.

---

[1] *GC 34*, D 26, n. 550.

HOPE IV

As discussed in Chapter XI, I would hope that Saint Louis University, as well as all Jesuit colleges and universities, would pursue diligently and boldly the challenge issued by the 34th General Congregation ". . . to develop the dimension of an inculturated evangelization within our mission of the service of faith and the promotion of justice." [2] *It is our universities especially that "have a crucial role to play in linking Christian faith to the core elements in contemporary and traditional cultures."* [3]

HOPE V

As discussed in Chapter III, I would hope that Saint Louis University would move with coordinated efforts toward developing a more professional support system with improved essential ingredients, for example:

a. *Coordinated academic and financial planning resulting in agreement on the part of administration, faculty, and fund-raising personnel as to priority needs for capital and budgetary expenditures;*

b. *Clear definition of the role and responsibility for fund-raising as between the President, the Chief Advancement Officer, and his/her staff; and the Development Committee of the Board of Trustees;*

c. *An advancement program that gives priority to long-range stability (e.g., endowment) and less emphasis on expansion and physical improvements;*

d. *Most importantly, a University support system that is an integral part of the mission of Saint Louis University, values fund-raising not only as a profession but as a Christian ministry, scrupulous about accountability, and consistently expressing gratitude for and promising spiritual benefits regardless of the size of the donor's gift.*

As we close this final chapter, the question haunts me: are these five expectations just listed mere pious velleities, or can we realistically look ahead with honest expectations? While I feel there are many natural and supernatural reasons for predicting that Saint Louis University will emerge

---

[2] *GC 34*, D 4, n. 109.
[3] *GC 34*, D 4, n. 125.

in the twenty-first century as a vibrant example of all that is best in Jesuit higher education, nothing has driven me more forcefully to that expectation than several unprecedented statements by Pope John Paul II during his recent visit to the United States. For the first time in any statement, Pope John Paul, in his address in Baltimore, praised the remarkable and unique achievements of American Catholics: "Since those heroic beginnings, men and women of every race and social class have built the Catholic community we see in America today, a great spiritual movement of witness, of apostolate, of good works, of Christian institutions and organizations. . . . In America, Christian faith has found expression in an impressive array of witness and achievement. We must recall with gratitude the inspiring work of education carried out in countless families, schools and universities, and all the healing and consolation imparted in hospitals and hospices and shelters." [4] This fulsome praise and endorsement by John Paul of the truly gigantic contributions to American society of the institutions sponsored or inspired by the Catholic Church will have a lasting impact on our efforts at Saint Louis University to build a world that needs to learn how to live with diversity.

But John Paul's second often repeated theme calls us from justified appraisal of past contributions to a vibrant hope for the future—a hope so desperately needed today. So much of his thoughts, words, and prayers went out to young Americans, not denying the challenges and problems of which we are all aware, but assuring them that by living out the moral truths about the human person and human community, they will find the answer to the question we Americans face today: "How ought we to live together?" Without watering down the ugly problems the young wrestle with today, John Paul spoke and sang in words filled with hope: model your personal lives and your service to others according to the spirit of the Beatitudes, all the while waiting for God to fulfill his promises, ever mindful that "God takes His time, but He is just." Possibly the most important single message John Paul delivered to all of us Americans, young and old, was the good advice in the passage from the prophet Habakkuk, which was read during the Mass in Baltimore's Camden Yards:

---

[4] *The New York Times*, 9 October 1995, sec. B, p. 15.

FOR THERE IS STILL A VISION FOR THE APPOINTED TIME;
    IT SPEAKS OF THE END, AND DOES NOT LIE.
IF IT SEEMS TO TARRY, WAIT FOR IT;
    IT WILL SURELY COME. . . .

                           (HAB 2:3)

BIBLIOGRAPHY

Abbott, Walter, S.J., ed. *The Documents of Vatican II*. New York: Guild Press, 1966.

Adams, Rita G., William C. Einspanier, and B.T. Lukaszewski, S.J. *Saint Louis University: 150 years*. St. Louis: Saint Louis University, 1968.

Bellah, Robert, et al. *Habits of the Mind*. New York: Harper and Row, 1985.

Bloom, Allan. *The Closing of the American Mind*. New York: Scribners, 1987.

Brubacher, John S., and Willis Rudy. *Higher Education in Transition*. New York: Harper and Row, 1958.

Byrne, Patrick H. "Paradigms of Justice and Love." *Conversations* 7 (Spring 1995): 5–17.

Daniere, Andre. *Higher Education and the American Economy*. New York: Random House, 1964.

Decrees of General Congregation 34 of the Society of Jesus. Rome: Curia of the Superior General, 1995.

Documents of Vatican II

Dressel, Paul L. *College and University Curriculum*. Berkeley: McCutcheon, 1968.

Eberle, Jean Fahey. *Midtown: A Grand Place to Be!* St. Louis: Mercantile Trust Company, 1980.

Edwards, Harry. *Black Students*. New York: The Free Press, 1970.

Ex Corde Ecclesiae

Faherty, William B., S.J. *Better the Dream. Saint Louis: University and Community 1818–1968*. St. Louis: Saint Louis University, 1968.

Faherty, William B., S.J.. *The Saint Louis Portrait*. Tulsa: Continental Heritage, 1978

"Fifty Years of Integration at Saint Louis University." *St. Louis American*, 9 March 1995, p. 1–32.

FitzGerald, Paul A., S.J. *The Governance of Jesuit Colleges in the United States 1920–1970*. Notre Dame: University of Notre Dame Press, 1984.

Gallin, Alice, O.S.U., ed. *American Catholic Higher Education.* Notre Dame: University of Notre Dame Press, 1992.

Ganss, George E., S.J. *The Jesuit Educational Tradition and Saint Louis University: Some Bearings for the University's Sesquicentennial, 1818–1968.* St. Louis: Saint Louis University, 1969.

Gleason, Philip. *Contending With Modernity: Catholic Higher Education in the Twentieth Century.* New York, Oxford: Oxford University Press, 1995.

Harris, S.E. et al., eds. *Challenge and Change in American Higher Education.* Berkeley: McCutcheon, 1965.

Kelly, George A. "Let's Stop Kidding Ourselves About Catholic Higher Education." *FCS Newsletter.* (Spring 1993):15–24.

Leahy, William P., S.J. *Adapting to America: Catholics, Jesuits, and Higher Education in the Twentieth Century.* Washington, DC: Georgetown University Press, 1991.

Lewis, Hunter. *A Question of Values.* New York: Harper, 1990.

McCourt, Kathleen. "College Students in a Changing Society." Address at the Jesuit Education in the Heartland Conference. Chicago, 23 May 1994.

McGucken, William J., S.J. *The Catholic Way in Education.* Milwaukee: Bruce, 1934.

McIntyre, Alasdair. *Three Rival Versions of Moral Inquiry.* Notre Dame: University of Notre Dame Press, 1990.

Maritain, Jacques. *Education at the Crossroads.* New Haven: Yale UP, 1957.

Minutes of the Meetings of the Board of Trustees, Saint Louis University, 1944–46, 1948–1973.

Mumford, Lewis. *The Condition of Man.* 1944. New York: Harcourt, 1973.

O'Brien, David J. "Conversations on Jesuit (and Catholic?) Higher Education: Jesuit Sì, Catholic. . . Not So Sure." *Conversations* 6 (Fall 1994).

Primm, James Neal. *Lion of the Valley: St. Louis, Missouri.* Boulder: Pruett Publishing Co., 1981.

Ratio Studiorum.

Reinert, Paul, S.J. *To Turn the Tide.* Englewood Cliffs: Prentice-Hall, 1972.

Reinert, Paul, S.J. *The Urban Catholic University.* Kansas City: Sheed and Ward, 1972.

St. Louis, Missouri, Land Clearance for Redevelopment Authority.

Redevelopment Plan for Mill Creek Valley Project. Project MO R–1, 19 February 1958.

St. Louis Post-Dispatch, 1944–73.

Schlesinger, Arthur. *The Disuniting of America.* Knoxville, TN: Whittle Books, 1991.

Schmandt, Henry J., Paul G. Steinbicker, and George D. Wendel. *Metropolitan Reform in St. Louis: A Case Study.* New York: Holt, Rinehart, and Winston, 1961.

Schulman, Lee. "Assessment for Teaching: An Initiative for the Profession." *Phi Delta Kappan.* 69:38–44.

Sengstock, Frank S., et al. *Consolidation: Building a Bridge between City and Suburb.* St. Louis: Saint Louis University School of Law, 1964.

Shore, Paul. *The Myth of the University.* Lanham, MD: University Press of America, 1992.

Shore, Paul, and Eric Daeuber. "Religion and the American University." *Concordia Theological Quarterly*, 53 (October 1989):241–54.

Toch, Thomas. "The Terrible Toll on College Presidents." *U.S. News & World Report*, 12 December 1994: 82.

University News, 1947–73.

INDEX

Note: For constituent schools and units of Saint Louis University, see as subentries under Saint Louis University.